D0934573

Hut Two

Henry and Betty,

Now you will learn that the Horn's were not the only crazy family. The whole Army was and Dad was and is responsible for the whole thing.

Enjoy the fond memories

Vic Warren
3/7/95

Warren Rangnow

Sharpless Publishing Co.
515A Woodland Avenue
Suite A
Cheltenham, PA 19012
215–663–1544

Professional Press
Chapel Hill, NC 27515-4371

Manufactured in the United States of America

97 96 95 94   10 9 8 7 6 5 4 3 2 1

Contents

List Of Illustrations

Maps

*T*his book is dedicated to Lester A. Wolf from Oak Harbor, Ohio. A farm boy who became a good husband and father. Before that he was a good soldier and friend to many. His spontaneous sense of humor always managed to crumble the ragged edge of the tough war days. Les died of lung cancer at the early age of forty-six. This book is a salute to his loving, unique personality.

Introduction

The neighborhood was Burholme, nine miles north from Philadelphia's City Hall. The address of my home was 7423 Lawndale Avenue. It was a suburban pebbled street consisting of tar and crowned. The block was lined with young Norway maples and two huge poplar trees. In 1936 very few people on the block owned cars. It was the ideal ball field for the 26 boys that lived in the 29 single and twin homes.

Three blocks to the west the B&O line to New York ran in a gully. These tracks were our hiking trail to the fishing and swimming holes in Pennypack Park, just a two mile hike. It was the perfect neighborhood for a group of fast growing teenagers.

The great depression was almost over. It had affected every family in the neighborhood. My Dad kept food on the table by going door to door selling metal radiator covers. Saving pennies was a necessity of life. Many a Saturday I couldn't scrape together the eleven cents needed for the Saturday matinee at the Oxford Theatre. We never went hungry but food and clothes were stretched to the limit. Hand me downs were never questioned. Our common dessert was bread and butter with sugar sprinkled on top.

When I started Junior High School a kidney infection laid me low and changed my life style. Little did I perceive this would determine the outcome of my war career. Gym and all sports were forbidden. My strict diet excluded meats and anything that was cooked with egg whites. These tough years lasted until 10th grade. My bed partner, brother Al, convinced Pop that I needed a second medical opinion.

Dr. Campbell was a kindly surgeon. He gently cupped his hands around my side, then gentle blue eyes met mine and he said,

"Son, you need an operation."

Five weeks later I proudly returned home with a 13 inch scar and my fallen kidney back in place. I had lost 10th grade but now I had a second chance for leading a normal teenage life.

It was late in 1939 when another occurrence molded my future. Out in the street we were playing our daily, after school game of two hand touch with a nine inch, 39 cent, football. Tom Winco looked up from the huddle.

"Uh oh, looks who's coming?" Brog Auch, Bill Irwin and I turned and saw a giant striding up the street. It was the new Pastor in town, twenty-five-year-old Pastor Henry Horn. He hollered, "Come on, let's see you toss one!" Thus began a long friendship that influenced many of our lives. Before we could explain it he had the four of us singing in his choir. Needless to say our infrequent church going parents were shocked.

Somehow membership in choir also allowed us to join the Immanuel Lutheran Church's baseball, football, softball or tennis teams. It was here that we built lifelong friendships. Fred and Lou Muller, Ed Perry, the Robinsons Orv, Fred, Wally and Sherm Barber plus all the girlfriends made for a close knit crowd. Pastor Horn was one of the boys with a collar. He was six-five, an ideal end for our Saturday football games at Burholme Park.

None of us Lawndale Street guys had a car. For 15 cents we rode the trolleys or walked. We "athletes" didn't smoke and cokes were the drinks. After a ball game and a shower our treat was a walk to the "Sweet Shoppe" to get an ice cream sundae and look over the girls. Sure dull by today's standard but we were enjoying life and the sports we loved while the war clouds were thickening over Europe.

By 1940 most of us were engaged in war work. Brother Al was a set up man at SKF. I always knew when he was home, every room was permeated with the aroma of machine oil.

My first job was making brass parts on a turret lathe. It paid $12.50 for a five and half day week. Early in 1941 Lou Muller persuaded me to join him at the Heintz Mfg. Co. For a five day week I was getting rich at $18.50 making templates for war planes.

December 7, 1941 was just another football Sunday. After finishing lunch I turned on our floor model, Philco radio. I was shocked to hear the Washington Redskins were trouncing the Bears in the play-off game. (Final score 72-0!) I had to rush this news to the "gang" who were back at the Jardel field watching the local football game. Just as I got to the door they broke into the game to announce the attack on Pearl Harbor. As the family gathered around, it wasn't possible to comprehend what we were hearing. "Japan has attacked the United States and sunk our fleet!"

I ran all the way to the football field. Despite my dry hanging tongue everyone refused to believe my excited recitation about Pearl Harbor or the Redskins. Laughingly Brog asked, "Pearl Harbor, where did you come up with that name?" By the next morning everyone knew the whole history of Pearl Harbor. It was apparent our normal, fun loving life was soon going to drastically change.

In 1941 Orv, Fred Muller and the best fisherman on our block, Howard Livezy, were the first to be drafted. I didn't relish the thought of being a doughboy. So, in January of 1942 I went to enlist in the Navy. It wasn't much of a surprise when they said, "Thanks but no thanks." My sewn up fallen kidney had let me down.

My draft notice arrived in June and ball playing continued all summer. Brog was accepted for the Air Force and Tom was a Junior in Lehigh. The whole Lawndale gang took one last fling in Wildwood, New Jersey. None of us were thinking much about girls until one wiggled by.

However, back in August, Pastor Horn asked me to do him a favor. The youth group needed an "older" person to take the part of an Uncle. The draft date of October 12 was my perfect alibi. He chuckled and said, "Heck, you'll still have two days to pack."

During the first rehearsal I was a bit uneasy with all these 15 and 16 year old kids. Then I began to notice one pretty girl who was a charmer and mature. Next thing I was talking to myself, "What the heck am I thinking? She is barely 16 and I'm her old Uncle, almost 21!"

It was the third rehearsal before she sided up to me and asked, "Rags, would you come home and help me with my math?" Now I was never a Boy Scout but I knew you should always come to a lady's aid regardless of age. The walk home became a habit but I never tried to date this Ginny Sharpless. The play closed and the kids gave the "old man" a surprise going away party in the house next to mine. The Lawndale Street gang razzed me for "robbing the cradle." I grinned and packed my little bag.

Two nights later I made my rounds of saying the fond farewells. At his request Pastor Horn got in on the act. We met in his car at Cottman and Lawndale and reminisced. His final words of wisdom were, "By the way, Ginny is one terrific girl; you would be smart to write her."

My last stop was the old Sharpless sanctuary at 7415 Montour Street. The goodbyes were said to Ginny's family and then we stood under the old pine tree. I rewarded her with a kiss on the left cheek and to this day I don't know whether she sighed or grunted.

The Sharpless clan were seven in number starting with Edwin at age forty-nine. He was an amazing Dad. Leaving school in 8th grade he became a reader and a self-educated man. He hardly spoke at the dinner table. To me, this was unnerving, but he was very opinionated on politics, war, and baseball. His occupation was Plant Engineer for the Swaboda Leather factory. This impressed me. They supplied the leather for National League baseballs. He would leave and return from work at six. After supper it was a quick cat nap followed by a trip to his fully equipped, belt driven, machine shop in the back yard. He worked until eleven every night, plus all the weekends, on war contracts for Coca Cola and Lucky Strike. Pop Sharpless was the smartest man I had ever met. He was the driving force of the family. It was my reason for naming him "The General." He never objected and the name stuck.

Wife Reba was eleven days older and she made up for his silence at the dinner table. She was active in church and did a lot of knitting in her old rocking chair. From there she would warn her young hens about the dangers of associating with older servicemen.

There were two sons. Bill at 26 was married, deferred and living in Lancaster. Chis was 23, already drafted in the Army, while wife Edie was in the process of moving in with the Sharpless' bringing along new born Kathy.

This left the poor "General" alone, in the clutches of six chattering females, and this probably explains why he spent so much time in his workshop.

Ginny at 16 was a barrel of energy engaged in so many activities but I could tell I was the prime one. June was 13 and the typical teenager, very talkative and into everything that was Ginny's.

The protected baby of the clan was ten-year-old Reba. It amazed me how she was always allowed to indulge in her favorite meal, bread and gravy.

The Rangnows resided three blocks west. Rudy at 55 was American born but he was a true krauthead. Quitting school in 8th grade he worked in the family business. "Rangnow Brothers" manufactured those large, brass cornered, steamship trunks. The depression and the automobile sunk the company. At forty Pop's new career had him traveling the nation erecting huge silk stocking machines. He was a hard worker with a good sense of humor unless someone calling us on the phone asked for "Rags."

Mary Jane was quietly wise. She met the challenge of raising three sons and Rudy. She was the typical Mom of this era. Mondays she washed. Tuesdays she started on the 21 white shirts that had to be starched and ironed. Wednesday was more ironing and a little mending. Thursdays you cleaned upstairs and downstairs Friday. Saturday was the sweet smelling, baking day. The big pot roast Sunday meal had to be prepared before church. Her whole world was in Philadelphia. In her 85 years of living the furthest she ventured was on her honeymoon to Niagra Falls.

Brother Carl at 29 was nine years my senior and he seemed old. He was three years married and worked in the Navy Yard. He was draft deferred and to this day he will still talk battleships to anyone who will listen.

At 25 Al had been my sleeping partner for sixteen long years. He was my youth leader teaching me how to ice skate, play tennis and the proper way to throw a left-handed curve. And, while working the night shift he coaxed me to teach his fiance, Mildred Grau, tennis. She, in turn, used his car to teach me to drive. We always ended up in the Sweet Shoppe to cool things off! How could one not love such a brother? Poor Al was not happy with his deferment. All his gang were in the service. Such were the times in October of 1942.

The years flew to 1988 and, while cleaning up the attic, I came across the 847 letters I had written to Ginny. She caught me sitting in the corner and promptly said, "Throw those things out!" How quickly love abates. Quietly I told her I would rewrite them so the grandchildren would be able to read them with admiration.

You are about to read how well I took Pastor Horn's last words, "Write to Ginny." Without Ginny I could never have completed the task. Her helpful criticism was most necessary but she also had the patience to withstand my constant questioning. I hope you can share with us the excitment of reliving the war and being made aware of the good and the pain of it all. You might likewise closely observe the mighty power of the pen as poor Ginny is slowly woven into the tie that binds.

Chapter 1

This Is The Army

The implications of the war were slow in coming. Everything was still " Over there." Our first inkling that we really were at war occurred when the German subs sank our ships off Atlantic City. Oil stains on the beaches became common. Then the first Burholme boy, Thomas Jardel, went down with his ship right off the Jersey coast. For the first time the neighborhood was awakened with the scope and tragedy of war.

There wasn't much complaining but now we started to feel the pinch of rationing. No longer was meat taken for granted. Rudy simply wouldn't allow butter to be piled on cinnamon buns. The first goody to go was Mom's Saturday morning breakfast cake. It was made with lumps of butter and brown sugar. The proper cutting area was located by holding the clear plate over our head when Rudy wasn't looking. All sugar stamps were saved for holidays and the valued gas stamps for a weekend run to the shore.

The high school day trip to West Point and a week's vacation to Wildwood, New Jersey, were the extent of my worldly travels. For me this Army life was going to be a real adventure out of some unwritten story book.

October 12 dawned clear and crisp. Carl and Al said their "so longs" as they left for work. The house was permeated by excitement and sadness. It was apparent with the passing of this day, so too would pass our normal way of life. I bade Mom and Pop a cheerful, yet nervous, fond farewell. This was the first time I had ever witnessed Mom with a tear running down her cheek.

Buddies, Brog and Bennie, crawled out of bed and walked the mile to Trinty Oxford Church. It was here that the 31 inductees had a short, required service. Ed Perry, our dimpled-face shortstop, and I stuck together like glue. We went by bus, downtown, to the Broad Street Armory where they swore us in. Another bus ride to the 30th Street station, followed by a three hour train ride, and we arrived at our induction center at Indiantown Gap near Harrisburg.

Our luck held as Ed and I got the same bunk. Ed, being much older, got the bottom bunk. We went everywhere together. When Ed got a shot in the right arm and winced, I did likewise. The only problem Ed gave me was he wouldn't let me forget the error I made which lost our last play-off game. For the few nights that we were together we were sure good for one another. We talked and laughed at the Army's crazy ways. After three days of testing we had no inkling of when or where we were going.

Suddenly, I was saying goodbye to Ed. Little did I know it would be 39 months before we would meet again. At 2:30 a.m. I boarded a train headed west with wild rumors of our destination. I cat napped until we went around Horseshoe Curve at Altoona. I dozed off. A loud mouth Sgt. hollered,

" Let's go; you're on KP! "

This upset me. I wanted the luxury of seeing every bit of this strange land that was sliding past my window. After dawn broke I began to realize this KP wasn't that bad. Our work was simple and fast, and it was "all you can eat," and the sliding car doors were open. This was great, leaning on the 2 by 4 that was fastened in the opening, I could watch the steam engine chugging away pulling 18 cars of anxious Privates. Dayton and then Columbus glided by. We had no inkling of our destination but there were waves of rumors flowing through the cars.

We KPs got the first clue at lunch. "This is your last meal; clean up and go back to your seats." Late in the afternoon the train was crawling across a treeless, muddy, desolate area. From the rear of the car came a loud shout. "This is it, Camp Atterbury, Indiana!" I had seen army camps in the Pathe News, at the movies, but this was like nothing I had ever seen. My day of anticipation went right down the drain.

As we stepped out confusion set in. They shuffled us from one gathering place to another. Each time some of the fellows were dropped and others picked up. Finally, at seven, they told us, "You're sleeping here tonight; grab yourself a bunk." We never got to know the barracks. The next three days were a nightmare of hurry up and wait. It was a shot here, a test there, then back to a test here and a shot there. Everywhere we marched it was through six inches of mud. At midnight, on the third night, in ten minutes I received my long awaited Army uniform. This also included shoes, arctics, underwear, socks, overcoat and a raincoat all thrown into our new teddy bear, the over-stuffed, Army, barracks bag.

Days turned into long hours of lectures on top of lectures. By now we were well aware this was the 83rd Infantry Division. This meant "fighting doughboys" and, while I respected their Pathe News reel image, I just didn't relish the thought of becoming one.

On the morning of our placement to a real Company, we anxiously waited. I jumped when I heard, "Rangnow, report to the 783rd Ordnance Company." I wasn't clear what this meant, but I knew it had something to do with guns. So far I hadn't drawn the short straw.

Just six days had elapsed since leaving the old homestead. Somehow it seemed like an eternity ago, but I was smiling as I quickly marched the half mile to my new home. The Sgt. took me to my own bunk and gave me my own mailing address. My Army career had begun and so did my letters to Ginny.

Chapter 2

Camp Atterbury

Oct. 23, 1942

Dear Ginny,
"Please sit down and I'll tell you everything I know and how I fit in. It will make a short letter. This 783rd Ordnance Co. is part of the 83rd Infantry Divison, which is the Ohio St. Division. It dates back to the 1st World War. You would love this Division. At full strength we will number 15,000 men.

Each Division is a fighting team composed of many different players. The infantry make up the majority but there are also four battalions of artillery. These fellows need a lot of support and they receive it from the Signal Company for communications, the Quartermasters to eat, and the Engineers to build bridges. The Medics keep everyone fit and the MPs keep order. Naturally, the most important guys are in the Ordnance. It's our job to inspect and fix everything from Jeeps to trucks and rifles to howitzers. For the present I'm learning how to fix the 75mm gun. So that's me, a Private Mr. Fixit.

Just in case they need help we must pass the same old fighting and physical standards of the infantry. They have gently informed us we will soon be hiking with full packs for 25 miles. I can hardly wait to see Indiana. Tuesdays and Thursdays are marching days. Other days we exercise from 7:30 to 11:30 a.m. I think the lunches are going to look real good.

My only complaint is my pin cushion arm. If I don't roll on my arm, I expect to live through the night.

> Your sore arm Private,
> Warren"

And so the letters began and continued. "Camp Atterbury is a huge camp of 47,500 acres. It has a nine mile long artillery firing range. The camp can hold 100,000 troops.

Our big problem is the mud. It's everywhere. There is no grass or sidewalks. After a rain this place looks like 'Boom Town' without Clark Gable and Lana Turner.

I can't complain about our treatment but organizational procedures seem a little odd. Every afternoon we march to the shop to learn repairing equipment. So far all we do is sweep and mop the floors. After five days this place looks more like a hospital than a machine shop.

You'll find it hard to believe. They have informed me my IQ marks qualify for Officers School. I just don't know. If I can't find a ranking here I might ask for a transfer to the Air Corp to sleep with Ed Perry.

Funny you should ask about my feet. After drilling for six hours Monday my feet were sore. Tuesday, I insisted on hiking. Four fellows, plus the Sgt., dropped out. I limped home where Lt. Knoerl chewed my ear for not dropping out. At the same time he told Hallock off for dropping out! So you tell me the answer. Taking the Lts'. advice I went to the medics. While taping both feet the Doc said, 'Private, I want you to go back to the barracks, and with your shoes on, stand in a tub of hot water.' I didn't do it. I could just see my boots this morning as two dried up, turned up, pieces of leather and Sgt. Jones saying, 'Why did you do such a damn, dumb thing?' It was the right, smart choice. In the same gooey mud today's hike was twelve miles. I made it with no problems. However, a number of our fellows are past 30 and they looked like the original sad sack.

'How are we eating?' she asks. I can't complain. It's a good chicken dinner every Sunday. I'm sorry to relate that there are no limits on our sugar and butter desires. However, my pies and milk are in limited supply. This Friday I have the honor of serving my first KP and that's a bad duty because the mess hall has to stand Saturday inspection. This means a tour from 5:00 a.m. to 10:00 p.m. It also means I must have my equipment and me ready for the early Saturday, Captain's inspection. I'm tired already.

Tonight's lecture was on censorship. We were warned not to write about Army secrets. I didn't know I knew any. We were also taught the history of the 83rd Div. In 1918 the Division was totally destroyed. First thing tomorrow I'm looking into that Air Force transfer."

By mid November the nights were icy but our hikes were still in icky mud. "Every step I took today was a slip and a slide. My 'football' knee started to pull. By hikes end I thought I was pulling the whole Company. This got me an ambulance ride, a three hour wait, to be told, 'It's just a little ligament pull.' The good news, well, I'm excused for the next two hikes.

Your weak knee Private,"

The first 13 weeks of basic training very few passes were issued. So they made Saturday afternoons playtime.

"Today we wore 16 oz. boxing gloves. We tried knocking off one another's ears. This was followed by a piggy back race, tug of war and an obstacle course. It was over and under all the chairs and desks in the garage. Seven of us finished. Four fellows went to the hospital with split lips and smashed hands. I guess the water's off my knee!"

It didn't take us long to learn that Indiana gets a bit cold and windy in December. "It was too darn cold to hike today but then nobody asked me. The sky was clear and blue but the wind was blowing so hard that after the first 50 yards we had a complete white out. Five minutes later the Lt. found four of the fellows with frostbitten faces. At mile six Lt. Knoerl hollered through the howling wind.

'Rangnow, grab your nose!' Quick as a flash I grabbed it before it fell. On returning, the barracks thermometer read five below; already I am praying hard for spring.

Some days the close order drills with push ups and a little shouting causes mind wandering to set in.

I had 'one of those days.' We have a little squirt of a 2nd Lt. He has held this title for 17 years! This alone tells you plenty. We were standing at ease and he sneaks his face right up to mine and hollers, 'What's your second general order, soldier?' After recovering my eyeballs I supplied the right answer. He snapped right back, spitting in my face, 'Weren't you ever taught to come to attention when you address an officer?' Oops! Jumping to attention I loudly hollered, 'Yes Sir!' He snapped right back, 'Well why in the hell didn't you do it?' Now I lost my cool. I looked down and stared him right in the eye. Bad move, it created a scream.

'You dumb, son of a bitch. Keep your eyes straight to the front. I'm not going anywhere!' He lied because he turned and strutted away like the cocky, little rooster he is.

After lunch he chewed me out for chewing gum in ranks. He didn't appreciate our sloppy drilling so he took over for the Sgt. He threw everything in the manual at us. In ten minutes he gigged five guys for three days. He had two others double timing it down the road. It wasn't the time to let your mind wander. Somehow, I did a dimwitted right face then had a red face. He was on me like a hawk.

'You really are a dumb, son of a bitch!' That sounded familiar. Turning, he walked into the field and quickly came back with a two foot section of shingle. Placing it in my left hand he quietly gave me instructions that I now had the pleasure of carrying it everywhere I went, including the PX, until sundown.

In civilian life Friday was the best day of the week, it wasn't in the Army. Friday was cleanup night. With chow over we ripped the barracks apart. Everything from one side of the barracks was placed in the other half. The floor was swept, buckets of soapy water followed by fresh were thrown everywhere. As this was being swept clean another team was 'washing' the windows with newspapers. The weather also played its part. Freezing winds with all the doors and windows open made everyone a fast mover. By 8:30 the barracks were back in shape. Now was the time to get your clothes rack straight, your shoes shined and your rifle spotless. Many a Saturday morning the floors were still dangerous with patches of ice.

After breakfast there was no fooling around. Beds had to be made tight enough to bounce the Captain's quarter. Our foot lockers were impeccable. Lastly, we are in our Sunday

best standing in two neat rows by our foot lockers as the
Captain and 1st. Sgt. Jones enter. The Captain checks every
nook and corner to the knots in our ties. One gig and you're
confined for the weekend. Too many gigs and the whole
barracks got grounded. When Jim Jones finally calls out, "At
ease!" you hear a whistling sigh of relief, for that means the
Captain has left.

Christmas Day
"Dear Santa,
As I sit on my bunk and look at all your gifts, I am at a loss
for words. I wonder, did you ever have chocolate candy for
breakfast? This is one Christmas that I will long remember.
A dozen of us made it seem a little more like Christmas. We
went to church and sang carols.

I opened my saved packages but not without a razzing
from Doggett. Somehow I received a package from 'The
Burholme Knitting Circle.' Doggett chimed in.

'Rags, you're not fooling me. Those girls are eighteen." As
I started to sing "White Christmas" Wolf countered, 'Rags,
would you try whistling?"

It was early in January as we entered the final phase of basic
training. This meant camping out in the woods and qualify-
ing with the 1917 Enfield rifle. A meager shooting experience was all I had with a few 22s in Tom Winco's cellar. My
anticipation of the rifle range was somewhere between naive
and anxious.

"This was a nice day to spend on the range, the gas range.
I shivered all day but somehow I managed to hold the rifle
still long enough to score 79 out of 100. I was flabbergasted.
My score was higher than the Sgt's. and the Officers. Wolf
had some words of wisdom for me,

'Rags, you better stop that right now or they'll move your ass over to the infantry.'"

A week later I wrote, "This man's Army isn't so bad after all. To commemorate my birthday they gave me the day off. It snowed and hailed all day yesterday while I was trying to qualify with my Springfield rifle. It was the hardest, longest day I have ever spent outside. My score of 148 out of 200 wasn't great but I was just one of three who managed to qualify. I have a black eye to prove it. Half the Company had trouble getting 110 so today, as my reward, I was ELECTED room orderly. Poor Wolf and Doggett are out there again today freezing their butts off. Like Christmas, I'll never forget my 21st birthday."

****

Chapter 3

Full Fledged Soldiers

In mid-January of 1943 we completed our thirteen weeks of basics. We were full fledged soldiers. Next was learning the full meaning of a division Ordnance Company.

At full roster we were 150 men strong. The Company was divided into sections. Automotive was the largest, followed by Supply, then Armament and Ammunition. These departments were self-explanatory. Automotive fixed anything that had wheels. Supply found all the needed parts for everything. Armament repaired rifles, howitzers, all instruments plus optics. To get all this know-how we had numerous men in special schools all across the country. While all this was going on we were supposed to stay physically fit with hikes and cold bivouacs.

My problem was one of frustration. I couldn't find any place to fit in. When I was discharged I learned one of the reasons. My civilian occupation was listed as a 'Loom Builder!' Most of our Sergeants had been in the service a year or two. They had more civilian experience and service time. The Company roster only called for about 10 Privates and I didn't want that honor.

"I'm writing from Valley Forge but as yet I haven't seen George. We are camped in deep woods and last night I had the pleasure of sleeping out for the first time in my short life. Yesterday afternoon was warm but then the sun went down. After supper we dunked our mess kits in boiling water for germs sake. Before we made it to the woods the kits were a sheet of ice.

At 6:44 Hallock and I crawled into our two man tent. We were numb and dumb. Of all things we slept with our gas mask containers over our shoulders! We did take off our shoes. It was an unsettling, long night. At dawn's early light I raised my head to discover my feet, a foot outside the tent, covered with snow. With numb feet and chattering lips I shuffled to the mess truck. Breakfast was a combination of powdered eggs mixed with powdered snow. The eggs had a commendable taste and the steaming hot coffee, for the first time, was divine.

Moving logs all morning warmed us but by early afternoon the wind and snow were increasing. For sure we were dreading another night in our pup tents. Then out of the snowy sky came an Angel shouting, 'All troops back to your barracks!' As I finish this letter from my feather bed, I have taken heed that the thermometer is bowing at 10 below. How lucky can one soldier get?"

Guard duty generally came around every two weeks. It was an easy, boring detail that lasted 24 hours. This meant you were confined to the guardhouse. You never removed your uniform. With your Springfield rifle slung on your shoulder you walked your post in a military manner. The "Walk" lasted two hours. You then had four hours off to sleep, eat or read. The cold, 2 to 4 a.m. shift was the pits unless you had some action.

"We have two areas to guard. One is our large garage and parking lot and the other is the Company area. This is a fifteen minute square route around the block. At 2 a.m. I was barely out the guardhouse door when this car came roaring around the corner. After lights out you must challenge everything that moves. Flashlight in hand I stepped out in front of the car. It stopped and out stepped a Lieutenant. 'Identify yourself,' I calmly ordered. 'I'm the officer of the post. I think I'm a little lost here.' 'Sir, that is not proper identification.' 'Oh yeah,' he replied. He went fumbling for his wallet and dropped it in the mud. Now I'm wondering. I flashed the light around to see if he had a girl in the car. He found his ID card and I let him pass, but he had me shaking my head and scratching my helmet."

It turned out to be the busiest tour of my day. In all I stopped a dozen men. One Private was quite intimidated meeting a guard with a rifle. He considered me the officer.

'Yes, Sir,' 'No, Sir,' 'Thank you, Sir,' with a salute. The humor of it all made a cold shift pass quickly."

In civilian life I loved to ice skate. Being just a bit unconventional I had my ice skates sent from home. I did not bother to check out the next day's events. I went to the Indianapolis rink and skated all night getting back in the barracks at 1:45 a.m. Exercise hour arrived fast.

"It was double time for a straight half hour. Sgt. Jim Jones was so impressed with my effortless gait that he came over to me and whispered in my ear. 'Rangnow, would you please dig me a five foot ditch?' Noon came and I enjoyed the chow break. Dessert was a 15 mile hike. Again it was double time until we hit the mud. Our guys were falling all over the road, on their faces and on their backs. It was a sad sack of a Company that staggered back to the barracks. Hallock simply flopped on his bunk, mud and all, and stayed that way until morning. Jr. Levis and I were so elated about our physical well being we celebrated by taking another hike to the PX. We each consumed a quart of cheap ice cream. The next time I go ice skating you can be be sure I'm checking the schedule first."

In early March brother Carl asked me to be the Godfather to Dottie, the Rangnow's first grandchild. Three day passes were the limit but this was a great opportunity to get home for the first time. I took my problem to Sgt. Jones. He gave me his funny grin then said, "Well, it's up to you to sell the Captain."

Now Captain Braddock was a nice guy and a respected officer but he was also a West Pointer. Jones ushered me into the Captain's office. He had his head down writing. Without looking up he authoritatively inquired, "Tell me, Rangnow, what is so important in Columbus, Ohio that would cause me to sign this pass?" Columbus is our travel limit going east. Without batting an eye I answered, "Sir, I have received an invitation to a baptism..." The Captain's head jerked up in disbelief and in a higher octave he said,

" A BAPTISM; now I have heard everything!"

The Captain wasn't through; Captains never are when it comes to passes.

"Rangnow, aren't you from Philadelphia?"

"Yes, Sir!"

"Then who in the hell is in Ohio?" Out of the clear blue sky I blurted, " My cousin, Sir!" Shaking his head he looked down at the pass muttering, "A cousin, a baptism." The pass was signed and in handing it up to me the Captain looked straight into my eyes and said,

"Have a nice baptism, Rangnow, AND... be careful." I thanked him, saluted and turned on my heels. As I passed Sgt. Jones he gave me a thumbs up wink."

"So powder your nose, buy a new hat, I have me a pass to Columbus. After that...I ride under the train. Don't worry, the chances of an MP picking me out are slim to none. See you in a couple of days — March 29."

It was great getting home for the first time but it was a crazy thing to do. Forty of the seventy-two hours were spent traveling in standing room only trains. The rest of the time was spent with Ginny. This was our first real date and no question about it, Ginny was maturing in many explicit ways.

"Ginny, it was exciting being home but it was much too short a time. I won't try that again. It wasn't relaxing and we simply didn't get anytime to ourselves. Someone was always tugging on my jacket and asking how I liked the Army. Not one person asked, 'How do you like Ginny?'

Now the good news is Lt. Knoerl informed me I have been chosen to go to the Post School to learn instrument repair. The first class was today but already it doesn't sound so good. The teacher called in sick. Keep your fingers crossed for my new Army career."

Everyone in the Division has to have a try at the rugged Ranger course. We were so busy getting the Company working on ordnance tasks the daily exercises were nil. On April 2 we paid for it.

"It was fun until they blindfolded us and told us to crawl. They expected us to crawl through barbed wire. At the first barrier I heard the Sgt. bellow, 'Rangnow, go throw your body across the barbed wire.' I turned around looking. Surely while I was in Philly some other Rangnow had joined the Company. I flopped and instantly six big guys went running up my back. Did you hear my groan? It sounded like your Monday morning moan.

By the time I recovered everyone was in front jumping over ditches and climbing walls. I didn't find them too tough so I quickly passed all the old guys. A creek soon came into view. The only way across was by a rope strung 15 feet above the ice filled creek. With my legs wrapped around the rope I started to shimmy over. Ten feet from the opposite shore I dropped in shallow, frigid water. The way I figure it my arms were fatigued from holding you."

There was no stopping; you had to keep running, jumping and climbing the whole way. The next obstacle was a small river loaded with logs. A little fancy stepping was required from log to log while they blew charges spraying water. This effort earned us lunch causing Wolf to remark,

'Rags, I think this is our last meal.'

He was almost right. We lined up in World War I type trenches and over the top we went. Awaiting us were a row of machine guns firing real bullets. The goal was 50 yards away but inbetween there were rows of barbed wire and two more trenches. The guns were set 18 inches above ground level. Bullets were whizzing overhead and charges were going off sending dirt flying all over us. Everyone became an instant, wiggling, ground hugger. Some of the guys froze. Fortunately, I was slim but Rennie had a big belly. Back safely in the barracks Rennie confessed. He had soiled underwear."

With the Army you never knew what to expect. On April 10th they shocked us with 15 day furloughs. Rumors of going overseas quickly spread. To Ginny I wrote:

"You won't believe this but in my hand I have train tickets to Philly good for fifteen days. Please don't try to meet these late trains. Draw up a lesson plan for my instruction. You will have to educate me. To buy ice cream do I need food coupons? I know I have to go to the Draft Board to get my food stamps. Brother Al has informed me that I must place them on my plate or Mom won't serve me."

Furloughs can be like a vacation where the anticipation is better than the reality. My problem was everyone I knew was in the service and Ginny was still a sixteen-year-old high school student. My Mom thought I was running her too much and her Mom wasn't excited to have a soldier sweeping her off her feet. However, we did get to know one another by going to the movies and double dating with Al and Mildred. The visiting and the late hours had me exhausted. It was just a typical furlough. The train ride back had me thinking about Ginny and my new Army career. So she was five years and five months younger, she wasn't a giddy teenager. Brother Al offered his opinion, "Boy, how did you get her? She is a terrific young girl." My mind was made up. Heck another year and a half and this war will be over so she will almost be nineteen. That's a young woman! As the train clickety-clacked westward I could hardly wait. Little did I realize how extended the wait would be.

Chapter 4

Goodbye Atterbury

L t. John Norton was our new, acting, Company Commander. He stood about 5' 10" topped off with red hair. His occupation, a Massachusetts State trooper. He had a quick temper with a loud mouth to boot. On returning to camp it just seemed natural that he was the first person I met.

"God dammit it, where in the hell have you been? Your supposed to be driving a truck to West Virginia!"

I couldn't understand his anger. I was on time.

"Sir, my furlough is up at midnight tonight."

"Well, get unpacked and get in your fatigues."

The next day I wrote Ginny from the hospital. "On my chart the Doc wrote, 'nasopharyngitis.' Honest I don't feel that bad but, after that Philly run around, this is a much needed vacation."

This vacation lasted three weeks! It became a nightmare The folks at home didn't believe I was telling all and I didn't believe the doctors.

It became difficult to write anything new so I was glad to answer Ginny's request, "Tell me about your friends in the 783rd." I started with my neighboring bunkmate, Levis.

"We tacked on "Jr." because at 19 he is our youngest. He looks sixteen, is short, stocky, always talking and a jolly Philadelphian. Lt. Knoerl, at 24, is handsome, athletic and a fine leader from New York.

Reds Rennie and Art Doggett both are 29 from Baltimore. Reds is happy go lucky and my unpaid advisor. He sleeps to my right and gives advice on my friendships and what I should do to get ahead in this Army. 'Old Dog,' or Doggett, is in a class by himself. Another talker and a funny braggart who hates anything physical. Hikes would be dull without him. Dog is in a class by himself. Nightly he tries to paint the town red. He is an honest and true friend who adds humor to every day.

My nurse, 'Cute Stuff,' thinks I'm stuck in here because the Company has been out in the woods for two soggy weeks. I'm so sick I have just finished three sweaty hours of table tennis trying to regain my physical prowess.

I returned just in time for the Captain's rounds. In our ward his visit consumes two hours. It's boring; you must stay in bed and maintain silence. Taking out your requested sketch of nurse 'Cute Stuff' I pretended to draw. When the Captain turned his back I got her attention. Then I held up the drawing, she gasped, and the Captain wheeled around to catch me star gazing. Poor nursey giggled and the Captain inquired, 'What is so funny?' Cute Stuff told on me! The Captain marched over and grabbed my rendition of Cute Stuff. I explained it was a little out of proportion; he replied,

'Yes, I would say so but in the right places.' He picked up my chart, studied it a minute and said,

'Lt., get his discharge. This Private is not sick!'"

Carrying my barracks bag I was quietly walking down the middle of the quarters, toward my bunk, when I heard Dog's southern drawl.

'Man I hope you didn't catch one of those sexual diseases in Philadelphia.' Rennie chimed in with, 'God, I got another raw recruit to train!' For sure I'm 'back home' and it's a good feeling. Already I heard the first hot rumor. We're going on desert maneuvers and then to the Pacific."

My new Army career came to a complete halt. After one day in school they disbanded the class. Rennie had a lot to say about that and the fact that I turned down a good offer by Lt.Knoerl to become a Company Clerk.

"How could you turn down two stripes?" Rennie griped.

"That's easy," I replied. "I can't type and I'm not one to sit on Jones's lap."

The Lt. transferred me to the Artillery Section and asked me to be patient.

My new boss was Staff Sgt. Bill Litrenta from my home town. He was a stocky, loud Italian, who didn't command respect. Rennie always began and ended his name with "that son of a bitch!" He gave me the job of driving a Generator truck. This entitled me to name her. On her dull side panels "Gin Ricky" soon appeared. Ginny said that was what she always wanted, "to be named after a truck."

June of 1943 rolled around and we were spending most of our time inspecting the Division's equipment. We went in teams and it was good duty. No Company Commander wanted his Company gigged so even this little Private was treated with the utmost respect. Beside that we were always placed in the front of the chow line and fed two desserts.

It was apparent we'd be moving soon. In June Ginny also moved to become a more respected girlfriend. I breathed a sigh of relief as she turned seventeen.

Lt. Norton was now our Company Commander. "He was working at a bench when I bravely walked up to him.

'Sir, could I have a couple of minutes to talk about my future?'

'God damn it, Rangnow, you know better than to talk to me without first asking Sgt. Jones permission.'

'Yes, I know, but I'm mad.'

'Son of a bitch! What in the hell have you got to be mad about?'

As I related my tale of broken promises, he raised his eyebrows and listened. Then he yelled at Litrenta.

'Sergeant., how many men do you have in your section?'

'Sir, I'm not quite sure.'

'Damn it, what the hell kind of a sergeant are you?' They left to have a corner conference with Artillery Section leader, Sgt Harris. At 34, George Harris was a neat, calm leader. Puffing on his pipe he came to me and said,

'Rangnow, we're keeping you in mind.' I gave a grin of satisfaction, but Les Wolf expressed quite a different opinion.

'Rags, I think they just hung you out to dry.' Two days later I found out how right Wolf was. Sgt. Gene Bond joined the Company. He was a fully trained instrument man. Sgt. Harris was now humbly telling me that the powers to be had applied to the Army Pool for the second man. I was back to square one, a truck driver and a handyman.

There was one Company inspection that, in spite of its humor, I couldn't write about to the girl back home. It's called, "The Short Arm Inspection."

It was bad enough when we had to sit through explicit, colored, venereal disease films, but periodically we were tested to see if we were safe to be on the same streets with civilians. The inspections were run off like a Nazi movie. It was always in the wee hours of the morning. The barracks lights would flash on with a sergeant shouting,

"Ok, let's go! Everybody up! Move it! Line up now!" Facing this sad looking line was a doctor dressed like an officer. Behind him was the Sgt., with the flashlight, followed by the Company Clerk who had a pencil and pad. Down the line they came with the light flashing and the officer repeating, "Ok, soldier, let's see you give it a good hard strip." If a dreaded drip occurred, the name was silently written down but the next day that poor guy was gone.

It was June 16, 1943. "Ginny, do you hear all those guys counting by the numbers? Well, they are not drilling. They are playing that old NAVY game of 'Chug A Lug.' Working for the Navy you probably know the rules better than we rookies. Our version is to drink a mug of beer without stopping while your friends count cadence. Levis and Wolf were just here to hustle me to the farewell party. Yep, you heard right. Tomorrow we are moving out. Our destination is top secret. Maybe you can figure it out; 1st. Sgt. Jones bought a hammock and I followed his lead."

Chapter 5

Summer Maneuvers

"The endless convoy through the beautiful mountains and valleys of Kentucky was an exciting, educational experience for a homebound city boy. The 114 mile trek to Shelbyville, Kentucky took us over seven hours. Driving through many small towns and Madison, was similar to being in consecutive Fourth of July parades. "The streets were lined with waving southern bellies and I think some adults. They threw us chewing gum, pencils, a few kisses, but most importantly, to some fellows, their addresses.

We camped on their fairgrounds right next to the last house in town. We are the only troops around so it was fun time walking down main street last night. It seemed like all the farmers were on Main Street sitting up against the buildings and whittling away. Others simply smoked their corn cob pipes keeping a watchful eye on the young, foreign males strolling by.

The town really wasn't prepared for us. The next night we couldn't find any food or drink. We had eaten the stores out of their stocks so they closed. In Woolworths we bought out all of their red velvet. They thought we were crazy until we informed them that we were the Red Army, with red arm bands, going south to fight the Blue Army.

Driving such a long distance in a convoy was a new experience for all of us. It reminded me of the old accordion player. We started out in a neat line then the truck convoy stretched out. The speed limit was set at 35 MPH but the different sizes of the trucks and the hills soon caused us problems. Rennie had a spunky Jeep. I followed with 3/4 ton Gin Ricky and Old Dog was behind me with his heavy instrument truck. We were supposed to stay in our section but it became impossible. Jake Houser, who was riding in the back, pleaded he had to go real bad. I headed for the near woods. Once back on the highway it took ten minutes of flying at 55 to catch Rennie. When I did the sky let loose with a downpour. This slowed everyone up enabling the whole convoy to finish as we started. Lt. Norton greeted us with,

'Good convoy men!'

On our arrival in Tennessee Norton sat us down in a hot corn field. 'Maneuvers will last eight weeks starting July 5th and then you will get a furlough. I can't promise the furlough but I will promise everyone eight weeks of damn hard work and long hours. We will become the best damn outfit in the whole U.S. Army!' Dog turned to me and drawled,

'Rags, what he really means is, this will be the longest damn eight weeks of your life.'

Three other fellows are now riding with me so here is a bit of their background. My assistant driver is Corporal Claude Sutton from Bridgeport, N.J. He is a quiet, unassuming fellow of 23 and is married. Rifle repair is his job. Jake Houser is big and acts like the Ozark, Ark. Indian that he is. He is a bit of a character but I like him. He sometimes smells like I think an Indian should smell, too. He's very well informed but with his incessant talking he can come across just the opposite. He claims to own 1500 acres in Oklahoma with oil wells. I believe him. A girlfriend came to visit him in Atterbury. She was wearing a long mink coat. Pvt. Atha is the fourth rider. He brags about spending time with the Georgia chain gang. His fun is trying to knock blacks off the road with his rifle butt. I steer to the left."

As we started maneuvers, the African campaign was all but over. Many Pacific Islands were being recaptured. Any big news headline started rumors as to where we were going. One thing was for SURE, we all knew by September we would be somewhere overseas.

During the first two weeks of maneuvers we were learning the routines of living in the woods. These are some of the humorous letters Ginny received.

"In the evenings we lay around the ground chatting and telling jokes. Last night a flock of cows got our attention as they wandered through the fence. Levis added some color to the conversation by swearing that last night he had seen a wild boar. Les Wolf said, 'In these woods I would say it's believable. We awoke this morning to an odd smell. We were surrounded by huge pigs.

This was the right place to try out my virgin hammock. There was nothing to it. Kneeling on my hands and knees I was straightening out my blankets. Suddenly, I went from a complete barrel roll into a nose dive. Jake too was rolling — in laughter — and saying,

'To be a true American you have to learn to sleep on the soft earth.'

Well, no sooner had I dozed off than I was pelleted with a downpour. I dashed for the shelter of good old Gin Ricky. Ten seconds later Jake came diving in. "Jake," I exclaimed, 'What happened to the true American?' The narrow wooden benches supplied a decent night's sleep, but I was stiff in the morning. Doggett loudly noted that I was the last one to stagger to Company roll call. However, when Jones ordered, 'Dismissed' I dashed by Dog beating him to the mess line. For the rest of that day he called me, 'Old Whirlway.' It's one funny sight to see 150 men, with mess kits waving and clanging, all trying to be first in line at the kitchen truck.

For the past two days our whole section has been making guns for the Division. It sounds noteworthy because we are using the best wood that we can find. Actually, they resemble the old rubber band rifles of my teenage years. The Army doesn't own enough rifles! Now comes the hard part — putting in the 'bang - bang.'"

Rumors were a big part of daily Army life. I always wondered how they started and traveled so fast. I didn't wonder very long. "Today the cook and I were returning with a Gin Ricky load of rations on a narrow dusty road. There was just enough room for two trucks to pass. As luck would have it an old man was walking, in the dust, on the edge of the road. Just as I drew even with him he placed his hands on his hips and Gin Ricky clipped him knocking him into the ditch. We were both lucky. He was shook up, but he was only scratched. After turning in my accident report the first guy I met was Sutton. As an assistant driver he had been worthless. While I did all the driving he slept. So I set him up by telling him my accident had me grounded for the duration of maneuvers. Sutton told Rennie and an hour later Sgt. Jones barked at me,

' Why didn't you tell me you were grounded?'

' Grounded? I am ? Who said so?' Lt. Knoerl overheard us and he said that motor officer, Lt. Kimball, was taking it up with Norton. By now I'm thinking how do I stop this thing, I want to get off.

Norton was out of camp. Lt. Kimball came back and confronted me, with his cool smile, and asked,

'Rangnow, are you grounded?'

'Sir,' I said, 'this is all news to me.' Summoning the Motor Sgt. he proceeded to ask him the same question.

'Sure he's grounded,' Kimball snapped right back.

'And who in the hell told you?' The Sgt. was taken back. Nervously he answered. 'Well, that's what everyone is saying.' Where was Sutton through all of this? The Motor Sgt., thinking I was grounded, had sent him fifty miles for gas. For sure I found out how a rumor works. It also left Dog, Jake and Rennie laughing tears and slapping their thighs."

The start of maneuvers put us under war conditions. We had to wear our heavy helmets, rifle belts, a canteen, plus our secret wooden rifles. Our strict orders for every new area were, "Dig yourself a deep foxhole." The trucks and equipment had to be fully hidden and four guard posts were on 24 hour duty. The food would be C rations. We were given offensive or defensive problems that could last from three days to two weeks. Sometimes we had the help of the Air Force and tanks. Overseeing all this were the Umpires who would declare the winner. It sounded like it could be fun but we should have known better.

By mid-July we were dirty and tired. Many days we would convoy twice, which doubled the work duty on cutting the branches to hide the trucks. We also tried to hide ourselves thinking we might not get picked to dig the essential latrines and garbage pits. But, if you missed those, there was always guard duty or an extra run for rations. Your name always seemed to top the list. There wasn't any fear of the enemy because our ammunition was all blanks or "bang bang."

Driving was murder as most of it was done on tiny dirt lanes, or across fields and through streams. We certainly caused farmer's damage plus a lot of noise. I never quite understood why the civilians were still waving at us.

Last night it was eleven when our convoy started to roll on a 14 mile jaunt that took three hours. Our only guiding lights were the 'cat eyes' built into all the tail lights. They are little, half inch, rectangles. At thirty feet you see four spots but, as you get farther back, the dim lights merge into one small, dim cat eye. With the constant dust we always drive with the windshields down. This isn't much help. You get used to not seeing any lights but it's tough on the eyes and nerves. Sgt. Sutton almost died; first he wrapped a towel around his head, then he put his head between his legs. His head kept hitting the dashboard so he ended up curled on the floor. This really got to me because I could have used four eyes. So I hollered, 'I can't see, I can't see the road!' Sutton popped right up, 'Oh my God, you can't!' For the next two hours Sutton too ate dirt.

The next evening we were sitting around hoping we were set for the night. I was attempting a sketch of the country-side. The sheep started to 'Baa' below us so repeatedly I 'baa'd' back. Suddenly, they were circling us. Jake thinks I'm getting the hang of Mother Nature but Dog thinks my case is hopeless. I'm sticking with Jake. He strolled down to the creek and came back with dinner, 21 great fish.

Levis and I had a neat guard post that was a thousand feet straight up. It's a twenty minute hike but the view is beauti-ful. You look down into this valley which has a small bridge spanning the river. We were admiring the sight when two bombers came diving straight out of the blue. At first we thought they had spotted our campsite but they turned and dove at the bridge. What a neat show. I'm sure the guys guarding the bridge had different feelings."

In between 'problems' we had three day rest periods and that meant, among other things, mail and packages.

"Lt. Knoerl came up with some moonshine so he threw our section a party. Your package was great. Can you hear the chorus singing? The Lt. asked me to pass on his thanks for the choclate chip cookies. He also asked how I managed to get all these packages and letters. I told him it was nice but not as great as it might seem. With twenty-nine males and females kindly writing I have a problem. I can't keep this up so trimming the list is top priority. Where do you start? Ginny shouts, 'With the women!' Hey, they are the ones mailing the packages.

Lt. Knoerl has passed his Air Force exams. This means I'll soon lose my best cheering section.

Can you imagine, Lt.Norton asked me to be his driver? I smiled and said, 'Thank you, Sir, but I would rather go to school.' He just nodded. Yep, there goes two more easy stripes."

The overseas news was getting much better. We had recaptured a number of Pacific Islands. In Europe Patton was beginning a run up Italy. With Russia's huge front the Germans were feeling real pressure and our Air Forces were now striking deep into Germany. Our consensus was the Germans would soon be on the run. The talked about "2nd front" in France will be the clincher. "This will start before we get there, leaving us with occupation duty."

Little did we realize the strength of the enemy. It was at this time that both Brog Auch and Ed Perry became navigators on a B-24 and B-17, respectively. My buddies were headed for Great Britain to get involved in the hazardous daylight raids. Our losses were averaging 50 bombers a day. I tried to imagine what it would be like facing that prospect of daily bomb runs into Germany. It didn't take much thought to realize I was plain lucky to be making daily ration runs in dusty Tennessee.

"This is our last day in our rest period. Tomorrow the Blue Army will attack us with the aid of Paratroopers. If I capture one, I'll mail him home to you. Rest periods are great because we don't have to hide. We're allowed to wear anything but a fig leaf. Today this campsite looks like the old neighborhood on a Monday. Wash is hanging everywhere. Lt. Knoerl informed us the guards will now be equipped with Bazookas, with four blanks, to shoot in case of an attack. The plan is to fire three rockets if by air and two if by land. A good Indian question was asked by Jake.

'What do we do if they attack at the same time?' At least Paul Revere had a horse. Stay tuned.

This 'problem' isn't starting out too well. We are in a lousy area of no creeks, no fish, rocky ground and no farmer's daughters. We do have plenty of chiggers. They are pin head size and pink. Some of the fellows have been running a fever, but so far I've been immune.

Just as I strung my hammock last night they called Levis and me out for guard duty. There was no way we knew the area. Going out we knew our location by the hum of the generator in the back of Gin Ricky. At 4 in the morning we had no such help. For 15 minutes all I hit were big trees. Please, in your next package send me a ball of string.

This morning everyone thought Jake and I were the best ditch diggers around. As we completed the two huge ditches, Lt. Norton walked by and admired our masterpieces. He then dumbstruck us with:

'Why don't you fellows take a Jeep and find a creek; go get yourselves cleaned up.' As we took off running for our towels and soap, Jake looked at me in disbelief. It took only a few minutes and we were back and gleefully climbing into our Jeep. Lt. Norton saw us and hollered over. 'You guys might as well retreat; that detail's been called off.'

Jake muttered, 'That @*(+%#!#$+!' It sounded something like an old Indian war call.

'Just think Jake,' I said, 'I could have been his Jeep driver.' Hmm, you think, maybe, the Lt's. sending me a message?"

Being an Ordnance Company we stuck to daily repair work and never got in any of the 'real' battles until July 28th.

"Jake and I were on guard when the Company started to run from the enemy. Luckily, I was still packed but, much to my surprise, Sutton had already run off with Gin Ricky. On seeing our extended thumbs a gas truck picked us up. As we thundered off the Paratroopers were floating in. It was one heck of a yellow, dusty ride. Levis spotted us as we jumped off the truck and yelled to Doggett, 'I got me two Japs!'"

Things settled down. I was tired so I hit the hay but as I dozed off someone yelled, 'Jake's been captured!' All hell broke loose. The Sgts. and officers started running around shouting orders as half dressed soldiers were trying to obey. Except for untied boots I was in complete war gear including my super, duper, wooden rifle.

We quickly assembled a flaky line of defense. Out we stumbled, forward through this unfamiliar forest. I came to a wide path and laying down in a prone position I cupped my hands under my chin. Now I was observing everything that was taking place in sight and hearing. Moe Debic was on my left kneeling behind a tree when he caught sight of two soldiers walking down the path. Moe was true Pennsylvania

Dutch. He stepped from behind his hiding place, and just as quick, two rifles fired two blank shots at poor Moe. 'Don't ta shoot, don't ta shoot,' he pleaded. When I stopped my snickering I realized I was now in the hero's position. For some reason though I just couldn't get up the nerve to return fire by going, 'Bang! Bang! you're dead!' So in a very authoritative voice I said, 'Okay, you got him but I got both of you.!'

Justice was not to be served this night. The enemy just wheeled and fired two rounds at me. After stopping the flow of blood I came to my senses. They, like us, were not wearing helmets. For this problem our Blue Army is helmet bound. Here we were shooting up ourselves.

This was too much. I was losing much needed sleep. After shouting for Lt. Knoerl and getting no answer I just took off searching for some leadership. Twenty minutes later I stumbled out into a corn field and again a Captain and his troops almost killed me. On exchanging the night's tales of battle the Captain just sighed and proclaimed,

'Damn, this is a silly way to run a war.'"

In the remaining weeks we became better organized but the sweat, grime and continual night moves gave us little time for ourselves. By August10 we were getting excited about the next month. "Ginny, there is good news beaming your way tonight but I'll tell you the bad first. Today, Lt.Knoerl caught me stroking Gin Ricky's hood.

'Rangnow, that's it. Sutton and Jake are taking over the truck. I'm keeping my eye on you; you are now my driver!'

Nope not even one stripe for driving a Lt. However, the Lt. informed me the second instrument rating would be mine as soon as I finished schooling in Aberdeen, Maryland!!!

The 83rd Division is also headed back to Camp Breckenridge, Ky., which is near Owensboro, Ky. A furlough in the month of September is now a reality.

Reading between the lines it looks like we will be in the States for the rest of this year. Now try to stay calm. Your hair is fine and so is your hat."

Our last move was on August 30th to Springfield just 30 miles outside of Nashville. Our fighting 83rd had the whole town surrounded. Every night the people would come by and stand three deep to get a look at our tent city. This gave the Command an opportunity to put on a good show for the taxpayers. Every Company went back to the basics of training. Reveille was at 6:30, followed by close order drill and then callisthenics. Before dinner it was full dress and a colorful retreat for our citizens.

Rumors were coming from everywhere. One had us in Alaska by Christmas while another one was, "Your hiking yourselves back to Camp Breckenridge."

A funny thing happened to half the Division. They did march the fifty plus miles to Camp Breckenbridge while the other half went on furlough.

My furlough started on September 2nd without the hike.

****

Chapter 6

The Furlough

FURLOUGH was a wartime magic word. It was a dream come true to get a glimpse of home life again! For sure, like everything else, you had to pay your dues first. With my train ticket in hand I jumped off the truck at the train station. What an astounding sight to behold. What good is a train ticket if you can't get into the station. Every soldier in Tennessee wanted a train home.

It was late afternoon when I managed to squeeze my way on a Richmond bound train. Of course, there were no seats. We stood like sardines in a can. When the train rocked we all swayed in chorus. It was impossible to fall down. In Richmond I dreaded the thought of changing trains mainly because I also had to change stations.

By the next afternoon I was pooped but I was home. Everything changed in an instant; it was almost like a child's feelings on a Christmas morning. Everyone was smiling, everybody was happy and no matter who you met they were eager to talk to you. I was amazed; everyone wanted to hear this Private's opinion of the war.

And then, of course, there was Ginny. I was fast closing on 22 and going overseas. I knew Ginny was still a girl of 17 who wrote great letters. Writing letters and becoming chummy was easy. Now, I was both eager and just a little fearful of facing the real facts. Would we just remain pen pals or was this a meaningful relationship? It was going to a be real trial period for both parties.

After the first visit there was no question. Ginny had grown in mind and body! She was doing well in her senior year and working for the Navy Depot in the summer. Ginny's family treated me royally. My Mom had a little different view. She thought Ginny was wonderful but she warned me.

"Just be careful you don't overdo it."

On the other hand General Pop Sharpless and I had many an interesting conversation on Army training and the war. Howbeit, when I asked his permission to take his young, virgin daughter to the seashore for the weekend his eyes sort of squinted and he said,"

"Hmm, Warren, I'll think on that one."

The plan was solid. Brother Al and Mildred had invited us and Lou Muller was on leave with his bride Ethel. The six of us just wanted one last fling. My Mom gave me a lot of support with, "No comment; I'm not Ginny's mother." What saved the day was the "General's" support for servicemen. Also, it was mentioned that Lou's Mom was residing at the boarding house. That was the deciding factor.

With a warm ocean and perfect weather it was truly a magical weekend. When Mom Muller retired for the night Ginny and I would take over her porch swing. This was the ideal process to solidify a young relationship and end a great furlough. For everyone these were cloud nine days.

Two days later Ginny accompanied me and my huge duffel bag to the old, center city, B&O station. Because I came right from maneuvers I was carrying every bit of uniform and shoes that I owned. To make things lighter I threw away my wooden rifle.

This, of course, was a sad day. Our farewell scene was later copied by Humphrey Bogart and Ingrid Bergman in the movie, "Casablanca." As I hopped on the moving train, I took note of a tear trickling down Ginny's cheek. There were no more questions, Ginny had me hooked.

****

Chapter 7

Camp Breckenridge

The train ride to Kentucky was a long, lonely one. The only good aspect was I had a seat the whole way. The last, long, leg of the trip was a two car, milk run that stopped every couple of miles. There were just a hand full of GIs on board which had me wondering if Camp Breckenridge was another hick camp. As the old steam engine chugged slowly across a large training area I realized I was entering a huge camp. Large Army camps are like going into a strange city for the first time. It took me an hour of puffing with my duffel bag before I found my beloved 783rd Co. They missed me so much that within the hour the Sgt. was lending me his rifle and pointing me to the nearest guard post.

By the end of September we were back to full strength and back to field problems playing hide and seek with the Air Force. They picked this time to test our vast knowledge of aircraft indentification. To Ginny, I wisecracked, "My system is foolproof. Our planes are white and good, the Germans are black and bad while the Japs are just plain yellow."

My letters to Ginny had to become more romantic. "Dearest Ginsy," seemed like a good start but it backfired.

Bill Appleby, our mailman, had mail call. Ginny sent me one of her rare post cards. Bill barked, "Ragsy Rangnow." From that day foward Doggett and Wolfe called me, "Ragsy."

There were many times when luck entered into Army life. Atha, the southern guy, who attempted to knock blacks off the road, got into trouble again. He was under Company arrest, awaiting trail, for threatening to kill his Sgt. and then telling off the Captain. I had the honor of being his rifle carrying guard. They rightfully told me it was boring duty so I stuck a Readers Digest in my jacket. While he was wandering, picking up debris on the grass, occasionally I would squat and read. Atha wandered around the corner of the barracks and Doggett whined, "Ragsy, where's your prisoner?" Heck, I knew he wasn't going anywhere. He was expecting an $80.00 check. However...the following week Sutton was the guard. He had to get a trip ticket for a Jeep and he left Atha standing outside the tent. A Lieutenant saw it and Sutton was promptly court martialed. He lost one stripe and half a month's pay.

In October, as I started my second year, the 83rd began advanced basic training. Again, it was mornings of close order drill, callisthenics and Old Dog, in his southern drawl, moaning,

"Oh Lordy, Mother, come and get me." We knew our supply classification was far from 1A. This meant we would be staying in camp for a long winter training period. We would have preferred being overseas, and getting it over with — over there.

As November rolled around, the command was pushing us to our limits. All the vehicles and the rifles were reissues. They had seen their better days. Our section had 10,000 rifles to inspect and repair. Everyone worked until ten at night. Physically we stayed in shape by being double timed back and forth, six times a day, seven tenths of a mile, to our barracks. Early on I noticed Lt. Knoerl would get on the tail end of the column and replace his double time jog with a runner's stride. My motto was, "Follow your officer's lead." The Lt. came abreast of my shoulder and whispered,

"I won't tell if you don't."

Lt. Knoerl was a good guy but the next day was bad news. He informed us he was leaving for the Air Force. He called me aside and told me to be patient, my schooling was still scheduled to happen. And so, I waited some more.

The following day we cleaned up at three and got in our Army best. Over to the parade grounds we went and stood for two hours listening to speeches. To keep our attention they threw in two girl singers. The government was twisting our arms trying to convince us to give up some of our $21.00 a month for War Bonds. I gave in a little; after all, I was still trying to earn a stripe.

One of the last physical hurdles we had to clear was the dreaded, mandatory, 25 mile hike. Hardy Captain Goddard not only insisted everyone had to do it but he also wanted the Division record. To his credit he led us and urged us on.

Off we started and I thought poor Doggett was going to die. His, "Lordy, Mother!' kept us laughing and moving. It was amazing, only eleven fellows dropped out. Somehow we finished in 6 hours and 50 minutes. We had broken the 83rd Division record. We were all amazed.

Most of the guys were too pooped to care, but six of us physical specimens went out to celebrate. We took in a movie and then had a quart of ice gream apiece. It was nine o'clock when we returned to the dark, snoring barracks.

One of my oddest experiences occurred on a Sunday night. Sitting on my bunk I was writing Ginny when the Charge of Quarters told me to pick up a Jeep and go get the Major at the Officer's club.

The Major was a harmless type officer. He was old enough to be my father and liked his drink. It wasn't surprising to find him a little under the weather but here he was with two nice looking girls, one on each arm.

"Soldier, let's take the girls for a Jeep ride." The young blonde giggled, "Oh, I always wanted a Jeep ride." The Major got in the back with the redhead leaving the blonde with me. She immediately complained the seats were too far apart and leaned way over to snuggle with poor me. Suddenly the Major remembered my name.

"Rangnow, put this Jeep in low and go across the field!" This was dumb and dangerous. At two feet high the weeds were hiding everything. Half way across I hit a gully full of water. What a jolt. I looked back. The Major was hatless and he was sprawled on top of the poor redhead. Containing my laughter, I helped the Major get back his dignity. With the help of the Jeep's lights we found the braided cap. In a toned down voice he said, "Let's speed it up and get back to the club." It gets down right cold in an open Jeep. The next thing I knew Blondie was throwing her arms around my neck and asking,

"Aren't you cold, Rangnow?" The cold air didn't do much in sobering up the Major. His parting comment to me was,

"Rangnow, your a real good guy. You stop in my office tomorrow and name your rating and you got it."

Back at the barracks Wolf and Levis roared and then Wolf added, "Ragsy, I want to see you walk into that office tomorrow. Smitty will say, 'Rangnow who?'"

The following day it was out to the field again for more shooting training. "Ginsy, you won't believe it. Christmas came early this year. Today the Army gave me my very own, brand new, 45 sub-machine gun. For some dumb reason I did quite well again. On my first try ever, with a 45, I scored 90 out of a 100. Here comes another sharpshooter's medal on my massive chest. Boy, I wonder what Blondie would say?

Of course a manly soldier, especially a Private, can't turn down the opportunity of driving a tank — for the first time. They pointed me across a high weeded field. My speed was around 15 MPH but the tank quickly filled with acres of choking dust and beastly noises. About now I'm thinking this is for the birds. I hit a ditch, my knee came up and kissed my right eye. My respect for 'Tanker' boys rose to 100%. Once was enough for me.

In the next field the guys were playing football so I went over to clear out my lungs. Suddenly I was running down the sidelines with a forty yard pass. It was our only score but I also caught an elbow in my left eye. Rather quickly I developed two beautiful shiners. Rennie greeted me with, 'Hi, pretty boy,' while Doggett's preference was, 'Hey, scarface!'"

My self-inflicted physical beating came to its climax while out on a cold bivouac on Nov. 15. When possible we could have a campfire but wood was now hard to find. Levis and Hallock started to chop down a tree. I went out by myself to finish it. In a few minutes I developed a nice blister. I turned around left-handed, that's the way I play tennis but not baseball. The second swing glanced off the trunk and caught me in the shoe. With a thick sole shoe I wasn't concerned, but when I removed my boot the little toe looked like it was just hanging around. I couldn't get the bloody mess back in the boot so I hobbled to the nearest tent, Moe Debic's!

Calmly I asked, "Moe, would you please get me a Jeep?" Now remember Moe was "Dutch" and a little slow. Gradually he raised his head and asked,

"Sure, anyding else I can get chou?" My reply that I had cut my foot didn't help.

"Dat's too baad." When he looked and saw my bloody foot he exclaimed,

"Jesus Christ, sit down." Out of the tent he went yelling, "We need a Jeep, help!"

A dignified Major examined me in the operating room and put it bluntly,

"Son, there is no easy way to do this." He was right but after he tied the last knot he patted me on the shoulder and commented,

"It's been a pleasure to work on a real soldier."

I felt like a real Sad Sack who had just blown his last opportunity of going to school. They said my broken toe would keep me hospitalized a month.

It wasn't long and I was hobbling and the Army didn't let me get bored. There were 1,246 patients in the hospital. I was one of three selected to tour the wards and wash all their windows. Friday night they would allow me a pass to return to my Company. I never accepted. That was their window washing night.

"Good Old Dog and Levis brought my mail and a hot rumor. They think we are headed for California. Something is in the wind because all passes and furloughs have been cancelled." The next day, November 24, Sgt. Jones called on the phone wanting assurance that I would be released in two weeks. My class began on December 19. I needed an officer for confirmation, right away, and none could be found. My cute nurse was a Lt. so I told her of my dilemma and asked her if she would call Jones.

"Awh, he's no good, no rank. What's your Captain's name?" Captain Goddard, looked and acted like an Errol Flynn. I was amazed to hear him chuckling on the phone at the Lt's. dissertation. Her last question floored me.

"Now Captain, can't you issue a convalescence furlough?" The only reply I heard was Goddard's laughter.

Three days later I was back in my barracks looking at a mess. My mattress was rolled up and all my belongings were packed into two barracks bags. My uniforms were going to require tailor pressing and I was adding up the cost when Levis asked,

"Rags, have you seen the bulletin board?" With this mess all I needed was guard duty, but my name wasn't there. It was right below the guard list.

"Pvt. Rangnow to Corporal-T/5-Rangnow." My pleasure lasted until Rennie's bunk.

"So, that's how you do it. You put a little knick in your toe and they turn around and make you a Corporal." Old Dog got in his licks with, "Ragsy, why didn't you chop off your whole damn foot, you could have made a T/4."

This razzing is what made Army life humorous. I sure didn't care. The two stripes would give me $16.00 more a month and the school in Aberdeen meant a Christmas at home. What more could one ask from the Army?

The Company had a new, business look. We were divided into two sections. One group worked while the other took various classes. This meant working until ten, three nights a week and then there was always Friday night clean-up.

The 2nd Army was inspecting the whole Division. Everyone was up tight about it. I quickly withdrew my rifle from the Supply Sgt. I spent the evening cleaning it. The next morning Sgt. Brown yelled over to me,

"Hey, Axe, did you check your rifle serial number?" Naturally I hadn't, I had cleaned the wrong rifle! Mine was packed away in cosmoline, the Army's axle grease. Of course, Dog had one of his usual questions,

"Ragsy, did the Captain pay you to clean his rifle?"

True to Army form my class was cancelled. The next day it was re-scheduled for January. What else could I think but, "here we go again." Ginny saved the day by sending me a pin-up of herself. It raised everybody's spirits.

Rennie, "How old is your sister?" Bond, "How much did you pay her for that pose?" And Dog, "No way is she going to wait for the likes of you."

We had a good mixture of fellows which was a necessity to keep harmony while living in the close quarters of a noisy barracks.

On December 4th we had an evening Company meeting in a packed dayroom. The Captain informed us, "the rumor of the 83rd going to California is called off." The reason? "Because of the Christmas holidays there is a shortage of rail cars." This was a puzzling explanation but most of us preferred Europe anyway. "There are no French girls on those Pacific Islands," was just one of Wolfe's quotes. In its place we received two more weeks of sleeping in the fields.

December 12th, I wrote Ginny, "Jones, in his matter of fact 1st Sgt's. voice, said, "Rangnow, your traveling orders are being cut. Your leaving for Aberdeen on the 16th. Get your things in order."

So "Ginsy, make sure you have the sofa reserved. I'll need to relax my wounded toe."

****

Chapter 8

School Days
At Aberdeen

The home folks knew I was coming to school but I didn't tell them the Army was giving me three days traveling time. It was supper time when I walked in on a surprised Mom and Pop. It was December 19th. I was their perfect Christmas gift regardless of how much of the time I spent at Ginny's.

Some of my glow disappeared on the Sunday night I reported to quarters on the Aberdeen Proving Grounds, just about 85 miles from Philly. The barracks looked like they were left over from Valley Forge. They were simple, wooden, shacks covered with tar paper. Lined up in each shack were twenty single cots. The preferred cots were those closest to the two, little, pot belly stoves meant to provide heat. The wind-swept Chesapeake Bay was only yards away. It kept the heavy, soft coal smell swirling in our faces so we nicknamed the area "Skunk Hollow." I was "home" but I knew the next eight weeks would seem like a cold picnic.

The school was a perfect interlude in my Army career. The course proved extremely interesting. I expected a hands-on mechanical repair course; instead, we received a basic optic course. There were two weeks of lectures, notes and drawings before we ever saw a jeweler's screwdriver. Classes were over at 3:30, then we were on our own. We pulled guard and Room Orderly but no KP. There was close order drilling and exercises every morning. Passes to 2 a.m. were easy to procure plus we were off every other week-end.

The hardest part for everyone was trying to stay awake during the morning lectures on optic curves. Three gigs and you kissed your week-end pass goodbye. I became an expert at staying awake plus a good sprinter. I was always running for a PRR train or a Philadelphia trolley. It was a new, different way of life, but it was still the Army.

While I had a happy Christmas the Army got revenge. They gave me latrine and guard duty for four days on my 22nd birthday. Then for good measure I couldn't worm a pass to Ginny's prom. She picked up friendly, Joe Schroeck, an old, ball team player. But I did manage to get home for Louie Muller's last pass. "That was a great time with Lou and Ethel and a lucky one. My darn train was so late I didn't sign in until 5:55 a.m.!

Very carefully I had made my way safely to the barracks and then I woke everyone by tripping over the coal bucket. Henry had fixed bed check for me by stuffing my cot. Now all I had to do, at 7 a.m., was to take my turn leading the class in close order drill. We resembled a Laurel and Hardy comedy. I couldn't keep track of my right foot and they had left foot problems. We were lucky that no REAL, Army Sgts. observed us. Most Monday mornings are like this."

And, so it went for the next eight weeks. It was either hit the books or run for a train. Classes became humorous as the fellows would nod off. One day the Lt. was beside himself. He started to sound off. He halted in midair then grinned and said, "Hmm, are you guys telling me it's my lecturing? Everybody out and wash your face!"

Having a good PX in camp also came in handy. "Tell your Mom I was successful, I found her Brillo pads. Now how do I get them off base? I got it! I'll stick them under my armpits!"

For some reason there was an Air Force recruiting station on base. By the seventh week we were tired of optic lectures. If you applied for the Air Force you got the rest of the day off. Henry and John also liked airplanes so the three of us took the exam and we all passed. It didn't create much glee for me because I clearly remembered flunking the Navy's physical. But then I made the mistake of writing this news to Ginny who relayed it to my parents. The newspapers were reporting daily losses of 50 bombers. Already my parents had me going down in a bomber over Nazi Germany.

The physical was routine and I wasn't a bit surprised when the Sgt. pulled me out of line and said,

"You've got to go in and see the Colonel!" Here was another Errol Flynn type officer. His feet were up and crossed on his cluttered desk. He was totally relaxed.

"Son, you have a slight problem." I'm thinking, "That's because you don't have my kidney."

"Tell me, how in the hell did you break your nose?" He continued with the fact he was a surgeon and he would gladly fix my nose on Monday. I was dumbstruck; my kidney had passed the physical. Now, only a little board exam was standing between me and the Air Force. This was something to be excited about. Hopping a Philly train I broke this good news. My parents were doom and gloom. Ginny likewise was luke warm to the situation. No one laughed or sighed when I added the plus of a new nose job making me on a par with Clark Gable.

Friday evening the three of us went before the board which consisted of six Majors and a Colonel. One by one we were asked the same three, dumb, current event questions. We did manage to get two right, but who has time to keep up on newspapers when your sleeping in the fields and running for trains?

They called us back as a group to face the Colonel. He was smiling.

"We truly appreciate your interests and efforts on behalf of the Air Force. However, as you know, you are now highly trained in a specific field and each of you gentlemen are prepared to go overseas. We must therefore deny your applications." Many thoughts went through my head as I saluted and spun my heels out of there. Uppermost was, "They should have told us ten days ago." And, "Doggone, I just lost my nose job."

Of course, my rejection brought smiles in Philly. Another hundred bombers had been shot down, certainly no smiling matter. But, Ginny saying, "I like your nose the way it is!" was hilarious.

After graduation we received five days of layover time. I was sure this was going to be my last visit home for a long time. Ginny and I made the most of it spending one day in New York with Henry and John's girlfriends. It was still winter, there was no extra gasoline and no place to go. So we enjoyed ourselves playing pinochle and eating ice cream with both of our families.

There wasn't much doubt in anyone's mind; our relationship was no longer infatuation. As the tune went, "We were two sleepy people, too much in love to say goodnight." It went without saying, the song was written especially for us, or so Ginny said.

Ginny's Mom sang a different tune. Every night she would send her song down the stairs,

"Ginny, let that boy go home!"

My great experience on the eastern front was finished. Once again Ginny sadly waved goodbye from the North Philadelphia Pennsy station.

****

Chapter 9

The Last Days

February 20: "It only took one minute for Doggett to make me me feel right at home.

'Rangnow, you dummy, you don't look any smarter to me.' He may be right because it's been tough getting the old hand into a writing routine. Our Army routine is right where I left off. Classes are three nights a week. Our constant warnings are not to write on anything Army. But I ask who would write about the boring, weekly lectures on The Articles of War?"

It was at this time that Gene Bond and I became great friends. Gene was a late comer to the Company who had previous instrument training that merited his Sgt. rating. He was single, from Lansing, Michigan and low key. Every day we went to the base ordnance shop, working with the two blonde civilians. We wore the jeweler's eyepiece all day long just cleaning the crosshairs on binoculars. It was tiring factory work, but it was the experience that I needed.

The Division finally got its shipment of the publicized Carbine rifle. Because of the light weight and small size, everybody loved them.

"I spent last night getting the cosmoline out of a brand new Carbine and then spent today on the rifle range. Can you believe, I scored 184 out of 200? I can't believe what is happening. Neither can Doggett who said,

'I don't care where we go overseas, Ragsy, but I'm telling you, I'm staying right behind YOU!' Our new boss, Lt. Gilman, gave me his ear to ear grin.

'Nice going, you just made expert.' He then asked for my submachine gun. 'Get over to supply Rangnow, you earned yourself a Carbine.' It also gives me a long night of de-cosmolining another rifle.

Brog Auch answered my letter in which I told him about my excitement of following him into the Air Force.

'I had the same feelings until our first bomb run. For sure my underwear will never be the same. That one flight eliminated all the glamour of the Air Force. A number of my friends have been lost. Getting the required 25 bombing missions and getting home safely seem a long way off.'

That letter, and Ed Perry's on his bombing runs, make me realize how easy we have it. We often discuss what hell it must be to see your buddies shot down and then the next day you're back getting shot at again. It brought back the Air Force Colonel's statement, 'you are prepared to go over-seas." Again, I feel lucky to be where I am.'

In early March Bond and I got a job of distinction. We went to every Company and inspected their instruments. It was a big undertaking but it was a good detail. The last thing the Company Commanders wanted was a gig. So regardless of our low rank we were treated with the utmost respect. They made sure we got to the head of all mess lines and got seconds on desserts.

"Can you believe, they again made Lt. Norton our Company Commander? He's not all that bad but his method of leading is cussing and shouting. Yesterday he was swearing at his Jeep driver. Bond and I were working in Doggett's instrument truck. I was mimicking him when suddenly his red head peered through the bottom of the door opening. He yelled,

'You dumb son of a bitch, you think you're a wise guy; I'll hit you in the head with that God damn hammer.

He turned on his heels still cussing as we all tried to surpress our laughter. Dog was quick to add, 'Rags, I think you got him this time, but you better not mess with him and his red hair.'"

Ginny had asked me, "How do the KPs wash all that silverware?" I replied, "It's unique. Everything goes in a huge pot of boiling water. Two guys pick this up and dump the water, then they spill the silverware out onto a sheet that is laying on the mess hall floor. Ends of the sheet are pulled taut. This begins the fun part. You try to bounce off the remaining particles of food and water. Each piece is then hand wiped using some remaining dry part of the sheet."

It was the 20th of March. We had our overseas physical; we didn't have to be told the 83rd was hot to trot. But, at a Company meeting that's exactly what we were told with the warning not to write any information home. Three hours later the USO was giving the 83rd its "Farewell Party." All of Indiana knew we were leaving, but we weren't supposed to write about it! There were long lines at every phone. So I wrote Ginny not to wait by her phone. She understood the unwritten message. Our time was up.

The Company had its own, sloppy beer party in the Dayroom. There were 160 gallons for 150 fellows. Most of it was poured on each other's heads. Gene Bond got looped but he was funny. I ended up putting him to bed, but it wasn't the best thing for him. Anyone in bed was fair game. The next morning poor Bond woke up, in his cot, out on the front lawn. He wasn't alone.

Two days later we marched to our 16 coach train. The orders were simple and to the point.

"Stay in your seats and don't even think of throwing a letter off this train!"

We had no idea where we were headed. The Pacific war was advancing on every new island. In Italy our troops were now beginning a march on Rome. The Russians were pushing the Germans back and our Air Forces were destroying everything with daily raids of 2,000 bombers. The much awaited and late second front of General Eisenhower, would end this war in two or three months.

So it was take your choice. Bets were placed evenly on the Pacific, Italy and England. The next step was to see if the train was headed east or west. Being combat ready guys we all looked to the sun to give us the answer. However, as we slowly wound our way through Kentucky the sun kept moving north, east, south and west. By the time it seemed we were headed in one direction it started to rain and then night fell.

Each car was guarded and it became my pleasure to stand on the rear platform of our car with my new, fully loaded, Carbine. We were ordered to shoot anyone who tried to run. This didn't concern me. Who was going to "run" off a moving train? No sooner had I thought it than we were entering a big city station. For some reason we came to a complete stop. In a flash we seventeen guards were on the platform standing by our door. It only took me a second to find the sign. It said Cleveland! We were heading east; now would it be Italy or England?

It was early morning when we chugged into a vast embarkation area on the outskirts of New York City. Spirits were running extremely high. The consensus of opinion was leaning toward merry England. Actually the French girls won out over the Italian skirts. Then there it was on the bulletin in bold print.

"A LIMITED NUMBER of six hour passes will be issued." Would they dare give me a pass? I sprinted to see the Top Sgt. Sgt. Jones looked up and, when he saw me, he grinned,

"Now don't tell me you think you can make Philly and back in six hours?"

"Philadelphia, who said anything about Philly? I've never seen the Statue of Liberty."

"Well, Rangnow, I'll give it to you but you better double time it, and don't be late!"

I took off running out the gate trying to find the right bus that would take me to the right subway and drop me off at Penn Station. As I tried to make the 90 minute train ride go faster I began to realize this was a crazy, young soldier's idea without much common sense. In six hours there had to be the successful timing of two trains, two buses, four subways and two trolleys, with a lot of sprinting to boot.

All this for a few last kisses and hugs. The hasty visit shocked the pants off everybody. The families were expressing forced smiles as they realized the finality of this short visit. I had brought the war home.

Ginny accompanied me to the North Philly station. Her face was somber and sad, but she managed one, last, brave smile. Little did either of us realize 21 long months would pass before I would again set foot on that train platform.

My pass was good until 3:15 p.m. but it was 4:15 as I dashed
into our Company area. Once again the first person to greet
me was Lt. John Norton!

"Just who in the hell do you think you are, Rangnow? We
almost moved out. Damn it, you should lose a stripe!" Sgt.
Jones came walking up behind the Lt. He spoke right up.

"What the hell Lt. he's back; no harms been done. Get on
the double, Rangnow; go get into your fatigues — now!"

As I quickly changed, Levis filled me in. While I was gone
they put the whole company through boat drills. Everyone
practiced going over the side and down roped ladders on a
mock up of an old freighter. I didn't realize what I had missed
but it did concern me because I was a "floater" not a
swimmer. We joked about all the German subs in the North
Alantic. It didn't much matter if you could swim, nobody
lasted long in that frigid water.

Our final needles were given the next morning followed by
a complete inspection of our personal equipment. Cameras
were not allowed but I figured it was worth a gamble. In my
clothing I successfully stashed my 8mm movie and a folding
Kodak camera. Now I was ready with time on my hands so
I dashed off one last, now censored letter to Ginny.

April 4, 1944

Gee, this is a whole new ball game, writing a censored
letter. Most everyone in the barracks is trying to write but all
I'm seeing is guys staring at the ceiling. Other than the
weather there's not much to write home about.

So let me introduce you to our dear censor, Lt. Gilman. He
also happens to be my boss's, boss's, boss. Yes, I have to be a
little careful. He is right out of college, home is Palmyra,

N.Y.. He is not as rugged or as handsome as me but he insists he is younger. All things considered he's not a bad Joe. The trouble is his name is Ivan.

Lieutenant, I would like you to meet Ginny. No further details are necessary as you whistled at her lastest photo.

That's it for now. I promise the next letter will be a bit more interesting. ..... So, Hon, as the song goes,

'When the lights go on again — all over the world — and the ships will sail again — all over the world —' Take good care of yourself and the Lt's. going to be doing the same for me."

After lunch we rolled up our mattress, filled our canteen with water and packed our huge barracks bag. Next we strapped on our full, back pack and slung our gas mask over the left shoulder. As we waited for the "fall out" we slowly sank down on our butts with our rifles across our knees. We waited and we cussed, and then we waited and cussed again.

The train ride to the New York docks was a short one, but then it was more standing around and waiting. The threat of the German subs caused the Company to be split up on three different ships. Dog and Bond went one way while Wolf, Levis and I huffed and puffed to the next dock.

Everybody wanted to ride on the Queen Mary because, with its speed, it could outrun the subs making for a short four day trip. Our queen was named the "Orion." We never heard of it, but it looked huge and it was British. The soldiers were barely moving as they struggled up the gangplanks feeding into the hulk of the ocean liner. The smaller guys were falling on their knees under the weight of the duffel bags and the incline of the gangplank. In this grumbling line of humanity tempers started to flare as first one and then another got poked with a rifle butt.

Finally, we were aboard and the cause of the slowness became apparent. Facing us was a steep, narrow, winding staircase. As far down as you could see and hear helmets were clanging on the low metal hangers of the dismal stairs. It was hot and the air had that musty smell. Deck after deck we descended until I began thinking this was a bottomless ship. Levis asked, "Rags, do you think anyone could make it up these stairs in an emergency?"

A loud mouth guy above us ad-libbed his thoughts. "Start saying your prayers now. If we take a torpedo, this tub will be hell."

As we spilled into our stateroom, we noticed it was about forty feet square with a low ceiling and it was crammed with picnic like tables. There was a great chorus of relief as we unloaded ourselves and our equipment giving us a chance to sit down. Again it turned into another long Army wait. When the orders finally came they were pure and simple.

"These tables have the dual purpose of being your eating and sleeping quarters. You are to stay in this nice warm room until told otherwise."

My visions of the great Atlantic cruise were shattered.

****

Chapter 10

The Good Ship Orion

On a troop ship one has plenty of spare time. It was an inbred habit for me to write these informative letters to Ginny as well as keeping notes.

A Day In April
7 P.M.
On board—?

"Let's see, how can we write a censored letter on this our second day at sea? For sure, our living quarters do not compare with the Ritz. For instance, last night, lying in bed with my hands clasped behind my head, I managed to hit Levis in the left eye and Hallock in the nose.

We are gently wakened at six and it's lights out at nine-thirty. Breakfast is a box lunch and supper is hand delivered on big trays. All I'll say is the food is not American and thank heavens for our PX with its goodies.

We have the run of the ship. I'm writing sitting on the deck observing the rough sea. The wind is creating a unique scene of waves and spray. The spume is coming off the tops of the waves like sand off a dune creating a greenish sandstorm. It's a picturesque sight for a virgin sailor. Many guys are sick. Right now the railing in front of me doesn't have a vacancy. With the meals we're getting I can't afford to lose one."

Our convoy consisted of fourteen ships plus three destroyers and a cruiser for protection. Whenever I was on deck I would scan the waters. I figured the Navy could always use another pair of eyes especially when they were instrument rated. On the fifth day, as I scanned the waves, the hair on my neck suddenly stood straight out. There it was, a periscope, a couple hundred yards to our rear. I blinked my eyes and it was gone. My eyes were watering from the brisk wind. Quickly wiping them I stared again and this time I found it trailing a little white wake. Surely the Navy saw this but then again they were a spread out escort. Two destroyers were way up front, the last one was playing caboose and the cruiser was far off port. Levis was relaxing on the bulkhead. I got his attention and calmly beckoned to him. When he arrived at the rail I was pointing.

"What do you see, Rags?" He casually asked.

"Periscope." I calmly replied.

"Get out.— Oh my God!" With that outburst twenty fellows immediately dashed to the railing shouting and pointing. The sub emerged to conning tower height. Our sub identification was nill but it had to be one of ours. In the next minute it dove from our sight and it left us asking ourselves, 'Now what was the purpose of that visit?' If the Navy was trying to scare the hell out of us soldiers, it succeeded. Also, if we were going slow enough for a sub to catch us from the rear, then we sure were not as secure as we thought.

April 11, 1944

"Each day is identical except for the weather. When the morning is dry we have deck callisthenics. From there we're on our own. Card playing is rampant as is getting junk food at the PX. Every other night a new movie is shown.

Our destination is now known and we are having lectures on the country's customs. It's beginning to sound interesting. And — you did get your wish. There are no WACs on board! However, there is a cute blonde. Every morning she is standing on the upper, off limits, gusty deck. Her flimsy skirt simply flies in the wind. We have no clue who she is, but I would guess her age at about — nine!"

April 15, 1944

"On this our eleventh day we are spotting birds which is giving us some hope of spotting land. The storms have let up so everyone is feeling better and getting anxious to see our new home. (All writing had to be positive. I wouldn't dare mention that the English food was too greasy for us. We were truly living on candy bars and PX cookies.)

Poor Vin Musser is so seasick he hasn't been up for a week. They are going to carry him ashore. At times my head has been woozy but I haven't felt sick. The secret is, stay on deck, take a deep breath and don't stare at the ocean.

The Navy gave us a little excitement yesterday. First we noticed the escort ships were gliding back and forth along the convoy. All the destroyers then dropped back and they kept going around in circles. The rumors spread that we had caught a sub but I didn't see any telltale explosion. It gave everyone something else to think about and a natural comment from Wolf,

'Where's land?'

"When the ocean is very calm you're not aware of any forward motion but there is always that constant "whirr" of operating equipment. On April 16, I awoke to a new silence. Jumping into my fatigues I dashed up the noisy, steel stairwell to find we were already tied up to a dock. In front of me there spread out a large flat city. A spirited dockhand answered my shouted question. 'Where are we?'

'It's Liverpool, mate!'

'A hundred yards in front was another pier. A ferry was drawing near and I immediately noticed a mass of humanity circling the deck, five abreast with their hands clasped behind their backs. They never missed a step until they saw us waving. They stopped, returned our waves and then they were off again. Already this was a strange land."

Chapter 11

British Soil

After two days of anxious waiting they finally allowed us the privilege of lugging our equipment up the narrow stairs. It almost felt good to be marching again mainly because everything I looked at was a view of history. The British train was made up of their unique small cars that resembled the ones in "Orient Express." The compartments were private and accommodated four people. Levis and I were glued to the windows. We commented that the view resembled a model railroad platform seen at eye level. Each passing town was picturesque and uniform with all the lawns and grass roofs neatly trimmed. From the two weeks at sea I thought my eyes were playing tricks on me. Never could I remember having seen a countryside so gorgeously green.

It was a short trip to our new home on the outskirts of Chester. The 783rd had its own camp, a city of thirty large tents. There were six canvas cots to a tent and the tents were lined in perfect rows. A wrong turn on a pitch black night and you were quickly entangled in a maze of ropes. Once we were allowed to visit the local pubs the rope maze became a nightly swearing pit.

The mornings were always chilly and it was tough facing the razor blade in our so-called bathroom. It was a no sided, tin covered shed. There was cold running water and we shared portable, metal bowls. They had one advantage, nobody lingered.

The first few days were spent getting us back to Army routine with some spit and polish thrown in. The only equipment we had to care for was our rifles. We were kept busy with morning and afternoon lectures on, "Keeping Your Feet Clean, British Code Of Ethics, Gas Warfare, etc. plus once again, The Articles Of War."

Getting to meet the English people was intriguing. We were surprised to learn their language was a far cry from Oxford English. To us it seemed like a foreign brogue. In spite of all the soldiers in town they treated us warmly. Every night the neighborhood would come out to camp and look in at the new exhibit in town. Everyone liked the personality of the little kids but they quickly wore out their welcome with the same repeated question.

"Got any gum?"

April 27, 1944

"Ginny, I'm all smiles having just received your neat letter from April 14. You ask what can you send. Well, how about fig bars, cookies and candy? Doggett just informed me that you can get any girl for two candy bars!"

Never had we experienced anything like the British sexual encounter. It was tragic because the girls were so young and some of the opportunist GIs were living the motto, "Eat, drink and be merry for tomorrow you die." Somewhere these girls were told that they wouldn't get pregnant if they did "it" standing up. You never saw so many funny attempts at love making. They were up against trees, walls and under the bridges doing these odd gyrations. One of our tent mates returned from Chester moaning, "That's the damndest thing I have ever experienced. I think I've ruined my back."

May 2, 1944

"Well, Ginny, let's test Lt. Gilman's censorship. In the next field, just 200 yards from my tent, there is a detachment of British Wrens. We have no buildings so all our lectures are held outdoors naturally facing the girls. It keeps the sun from shining in our eyes.

Today it was more aircraft identification. And in spite of the female distraction, we got the B17 down pat. Their airfield is close by and they are coming in so low we can see every detail of the shattered bombers. As I watch them disappear below tree level, I'm mentally aware of the anxiety that Brog and Ed face as a daily diet.

As long as we behave we are allowed four passes a week. Night passes go from six to eleven while weekends the passes are twelve hours. I've been to some movies but the theaters stink. Everyone is smoking. Never again will I sit up in the balcony. It was like trying to see through a London fog.

For the real flavor of Britain you have to visit the old pubs. You know they are quite different from our normal bars. These really are family orientated. I have seen Moms drinking a beer while enjoying GIs teaching jitterbugging. Last night I decided to try a warm, dark beer. As I sipped it, a Mom was watching my face and she exclaimed:

'Try the cider, boy!'"

****

Moving day was May 8th. It was to the lovely countryside in the vicinity of Nantwich, Market Drayton and Shewsbury. Our quarters were four quonset huts set in the corner of a lush farm overlooking a large pond. Every morning I enjoyed taking a deep breath to smell the earth and listen to the songs of the foreign birds. It was a serene setting for us city boys.

Our new training had us raising our eyebrows. We were learning how to waterproof our brand new vehicles. It was an interesting chore. The whole electrical system was enclosed and the exhaust pipe was extended up over the top of the roof. Using the pond as our testing area we put the vehicle in low gear, pulled out the throttle, and then hopped up on the back of the driver's seat. Steering was done with the feet. I was thinking I should have spent more time in the swimming pool instead of the ball field. The project was an intriguing one but it raised a new, suspenseful question in everyone's mind. Does this mean we are scheduled to be in the first wave of the invasion? Just a few months ago it seemed for sure Hitler would be done by now leaving us with the mop up duty. Now, there was no question, we were on the brink of the BIG invasion. Mentally we started to deal with this frightening reality.

Hikes became a daily routine but two things were different from the states. There was no mud and the narrow, winding roads created a series of wrong turns. Most hikes were longer than scheduled but were considered successful if we didn't get lost.

May 10, 1944

"Yes, Ginny, I have heard from your brother Chis and Brog. There was one clue on Brog's airbase but, after a long bus ride, it was a dead end. There's little chance that any of us will meet. Censorship is so tight we can't mention a town where we could meet. Passes are only granted for one day of a week-end. Last Sunday I ran into Joe Neff from the old neighborhood. We had tea and biscuits while reminiscing of our school days.

Ginny, you never told me how you British drink tea. I ordered mine straight. The waitress turned her little nose up in the air and remarked:

'How can you drink it that way? That's awful.'"

****

Just when we thought the Army was organized they threw us another curve. On May 10 we had to remove all 83rd identification from vehicles and our uniforms. May 21st came and they kept us busy by putting them back on. If they were trying to confuse us, they sure succeeded. This got the rumor mills going full blast. "We're in the fake invasion; the real push will be in southern France; etc." The people on the homefront were likewise trying to guess the date and place of the invasion. Ginny asked my opinion. "Guess what?" I answered, "I'm not allowed to write a guess, I could guess right. Let's see how the Lt. handles this one. The Italian front looks good now that it is on the move."

May 29, 1944

"I can't complain about the Red Cross. Yesterday I asked them about playing tennis. The little lass said, 'No problem,' as she handed me sneaks, three balls and a nice tennis racket. This pass was well worth the ride. A four block walk and here were ten, beautiful, green, grass courts decked out with 20 Wrens — in shorts!

Here I was all alone. What could I do but study their various forms. Then while I was looking the other way it happened. A cute little gal asked, 'You want to hit some, soldier?' I had a few ifs and buts but then I consented to humble myself for my country's sake. Secretly I just knew all eyes would be on me so I pledged myself not to show up this poor British kid.

After warming up I reluctantly agreed to play her a set. I lobbed my first serve and she hit it back with an undercut chop. I lunged at the ball, my feet went out from under me and I landed flat on my face. Oh well, it was early. Two points later she gave me a top spin like I had never seen. I swung and hit air! Now I'm really concentrating on her stroking and she is zeroing in on my corners. She ran me until my tongue was flapping on my knees. The final score was 6-1 and I was humbled. She walked up to the net with that darn dimpled, victory smile, extended her winner's hand and said, 'You played well considering it was your first go on grass. I do hope those bloody green stains come out of your trousers.'

She was gracious so I sincerely thanked her, but walking away I talked to myself. 'So it was a soft, velvet carpet of green; she was cute, nuts. I was trounced, who wants to play tennis in Britain anyway?'"

****

The next day tennis was forgotten as I was trying out our water proofing work on our new "Gin Ricky." Our objective looked like fun. All we had to do was drive our trucks to the other side of this four foot deep lake. I pulled out the throttle, hopped up on the top of the seat and away we went. This was a piece of cake until two Jeeps in front of me disappeared in hidden holes. My mind started sending me flashes. "Why didn't you learn how to swim? "This isn't going to be so easy if someone is shooting my way."

Most of our late night discussions were centered on the INVASION. It was puzzling because we knew many of the Divisions were older with more experience. Being in the BIG invasion never crossed our minds. Our daily lectures were now specific, "Drinking Proper Water, Gathering Food From The Land, Map Reading," to go along with many gas mask drills. No longer were there any doubts where we were headed. I had been driving the Major to many Army depots. My eyes would bulge when I saw the size of the stockpiles of our equipment in massive yards and warehouses. The level of our anxiety would rise with each London radio news report of, "No Invasion News." The whole Company attitude was beginning to express the same opinion, "Let's get on with it."

Tuesday, June 6, 1944
7:30 a.m.

"This is a funny time to be writing but I have a few minutes and, if our dear Lt. will cooperate, I'll tell you where I was yesterday. It was the funny sounding town of Rhosllan-erchrugog. You English sure pick odd names and I doubt that you or the General Ed will find it on your map.

The Stars and Stripes have a story that you had a false alarm on Sunday about the invasion. Boy, I'll bet everybody with anyone over here is on edge. Sorry, I have got to dash. I have the honor of playing taxi driver for our Colonel and Major.

Wow, now it's 7:30 p.m. and how fast things change. I was driving all day and the invasion sure caught me by surprise. I was having lunch in a mess hall with total strangers when I noticed their excited chatter. I knew something must have happened so I asked the dumb question, 'Has the invasion started?' The Colonel or Major could have prevented that embarrassment. They were informed on our first stop, but for some reason they chose not to tell me. Maybe they were afraid I'd get excited and ram a tree. Anyway, see if I drive them again.

The hut tonight sounds like a girls sorority. Everyone is trying to get in their expert opinion on the invasion. For us we are lucky to be sitting in this warm, dry hut. Being in that first wave had to be a brutal experience. I'm sure the first day casualty list will be viewed with horror. On the bright side Levis is predicting we'll be home by Christmas. His is a nice view from left field.

Brog has taken his B-24 to bomb Italy. His living quarters are a tent and he is washing out of a helmet. Who said the Air Force had it made?"

June 8, 1944

"Ginny, I hope you're keeping your cool head. I can well imagine the anguish our families are going through wondering if we're in the big battle. You now know, all of our outgoing mail, for the past two weeks was kept in storage to prevent any invasion leak. Before this war is over it is sure to happen again. If you don't hear from me for a long period, just remember, I could be on the move or the lid is on the mail.

Your comments on racial prejudice in the service are interesting. England adds a different perspective to the problem. This subject is rather taboo but let me try to get this by our dear Censor. The British girls were dating both black and white soldiers in the same town and that led to trouble. The Army solved the problem by declaring towns either 'Black or White.' Your newspaper story of blacks passing themselves off as American Indians is a wild rumor. The British are much smarter than that. I have seen these 'Black' towns in operation and, from it, one could conclude that racial conflicts can be eliminated. It would be a good idea but I really doubt if we will see it in our lifetime."

Every once in awhile Ginny and I would exchange our opinions on possible "earth shattering" subjects. Poor Lt. Gilman, if he saw me writing, would rightfully moan, "Rangnow, please, not another book."

****

June 14, 1944

"The radio is working again and we are listening to a broadcast right from the front. Oh boy, a real blow by blow account. The weapon firing is loud and clear until the whine of a diving plane drowns them out. The excited announcer is explaining what he thinks is happening and Doggett is groaning, 'Oh laudy, laudy, this ain't for me.'"

****

As I sealed that letter Sgt. Harris came in announcing, "We are on alert, check and recheck all your equipment and get it packed." Suddenly our anxiety rose a few notches. The deepest penetration in France was still stuck at two miles. A retreat like Dunkirk was an unspoken possibility. As long as the Allies were controlling the air and the sea, we felt sure of our capabilities. Heck, it would only be a matter of time before we had the Nazis running backwards.

At midnight, on June 16th, we rolled our trucks down the highway. It was pitch black with no headlights to guide us across this foreign land to an unknown destination. As dawn approached our speed picked up, and with that came an abundance of small towns. The sidewalks became fully lined with waving people. Our arms were weary from waving back. Wolf was driving and he asked, "Rags, how in the heck did England grow so large overnight?'

At three in the afternoon our large convoy pulled to the side of the road. We were five miles from Southampton. The Lt. said he was going to a field meeting for directions to our new camp. A half hour later the officers came back and the whole Company was marched into the field. In quick order we were issued French money, a dictionary, seasick pills, a throw up bag and live ammunition. There would be no campsite. Our fun and games were over. The Lt's. orders were to the point, "Gentleman, load your weapons."

It was another long wait until midnight before we started to "roll it" to the docks. We were slowly crawling through the center of Southampton when suddenly the air raid sirens blared. We halted on this wide eyed alert. The people were running and disappearing into their underground shelters. For the first time Wolf didn't have a glib remark. It got scary as the bombs started bursting. We didn't have many choices. The chills of war were running up and down my spine so we sat and sweated it out.

At the docks it became another all night wait. Nobody seemed to know any time schedule so we just milled around as they slowly began to load our vehicles on three Liberty freighters. This was a picture for posterity. As it became light enough I reached down into my duffel bag and hauled out my movie camera. I was quickly intrigued taking the shots of these cranes picking up our fully loaded, large trucks like they were a little toy. The spell was broken by a sudden shouted command.

"Get that soldier with the camera!" Glancing up to the railing I saw a mad Major pointing his finger down my throat. Gulping I turned and ducked into the swarm of my buddies. An instant later two M.P.s and a Lt. were elbowing their way through us. The Lt. spotted tall Sgt. Jones and asked him:

"Where's the soldier with the camera?" Without blinking Jones looked down at the Lt. and replied,

"Sir, what soldier, what camera?" A few minutes later they gave up searching. Sgt. Jones wandered over to me and spit out:

"Damn it, Rangnow, in the future let's be more discreet!"

The docks were jammed with many different units of the Division. From being up two nights, and now all this milling around, we were dog tired. A group of us found a five foot high pile covered with a tarp. As we sat down and leaned back, a bunch of points jabbed me in the ribs. Curious, I peeked under the pile and pulled out an object to share with Levis and Wolf. Loud and clear I declared:

"Here you are, pick up your GI issue.!" The joke didn't float. This huge pile consisted of hundreds of white, wooden crosses.

It was a K ration lunch before marching on board this rusty looking Liberty ship. Again, for safety's sake, the Company was equally split up and put on three ships. I found a spot at the rail and, as I looked out over the harbor, I was astounded to see the magnitude of the shipping moving through the harbor. There was no question in my mind the size and scope of this operation would never be seen again.

Moving slowly our ship found a slot in one of the many long lines of ships. Turning I looked in every direction and, as far as I could see on this mostly clouded day, there were ships of all sizes steaming for the shores of France. Many of the ships were flying miniature blimps. They were anchored by steel cables which deterred any dive bombers from giving it a try.

One look at the sky and I felt assured that we didn't have to worry about the German Air Force today. Through the clouds, on the right side of the ship, you could see a solid line of planes going to France. On the left side there was an equally endless line of planes returning. An opinion came from the rear. "These Germans won't be able to hold us back much longer."

Halfway across the channel the weather suddenly closed in while the sea rose along with some of the stomachs. It was then that they informed us we would see France in an hour.

Our stated objective was Omaha beach. Levis added, "Great, we'll be on the beach before we know it." An hour later the anchor dropped. We were two miles off shore. Through the lowering clouds we could make out the high cliffs which the daring Rangers had scaled eleven days ago.

The winds changed drastically as darkness fell. White caps now filled the channel. The ship developed a sickening roll and I was relieved when they informed us it was now too rough to disembark.

The bedrolls came out and everyone was looking for a place to curl up for the night. Wolf and I went down into the hull and found Gin Ricky where we nestled up for the night hoping for a sunny dawn.

Early the next morning we struggled up top with woozy heads. The ceiling was zero and wind and sea were higher than yesterday. Much later I sat down and started a daily diary.

"Morning Three. Frustration and doubt are setting in. The sea just keeps rolling. The visibility is so poor I can't see the ship next to us. Our K rations ran out so we climbed down to the trucks and dug out the 10 in 1 rations. This is a wee bit better but half the fellows are too sick to care."

"Morning Four. Our spirits rose with the lifting fog. Some of our infantry are disembarking. It's hard to see but it appears they made it ok. Moe Debic has provided us with some comic relief. He appeared suddenly, went over the rail and down a rope, stark naked. Now he is clean and has his bragging rights of swimming in the channel. My camera — it's tucked away in Gin Ricky. Later in the day, because of the wave heights, they stopped all landings. Gloom has returned.

Last night for the first time we saw the front. It was quite a show. The sky was lighting up like bursting, hot lava. Levis and I stayed up and watched the fireworks. Near midnight one German plane flew over. Tracer bullets formed perfect, colored arcs but they had no damaging effect."

"Day Six. Boy, this is some experience. This channel doesn't look that rough to me and each day drags on into the next. The sky has not cleared; there is a constant, lousy drizzle. Not one ship has disembarked. Many fellows are still sick and not eating. I can't imagine being an infantry man under these conditions and then having to go ashore and fight. Just for something to do some guys have cleaned, and then recleaned, their rifles. This ship was not loaded with the thought that it was going to harbor troops for this long period. These close quarters are a bit much. It's no wonder that we're starting to get on one another's nerves. One has to be careful about joking around. At least Wolf and I don't have that problem. We laugh with one another."

"Day Seven. Had us a little diversion. Our Division Commander, General Macon, is on board with ME. By shouting and waving his arms he finally got the attention of a passing landing craft. As the boat drew close the General hollered down to the officer on board. I heard one clear statement from the General:

"I don't care, I want off this God damn ship!" That exchange gave us a needed laugh but it also informed me that we and the General were in the same boat — frustrated.

It took until noon Saturday, June 24th, before we finally got the orders, "Prepare to disembark." The white caps were gone and I had the feeling that this would be a piece of cake for a non-swimmer. The first two landing craft that pulled up to our side quickly changed my mind. These little ships were bouncing in and then rolling away from our ship. With much interest I watched the first two fellows as they hesitantly lowered themselves down the thick rope webbing. Standing in the landing craft were two big "catchers." They were informing these fellows that when they heard, "NOW!" they were to jump immediately. To make matters worse you had to face the rope ladder forcing you to jump off backwards. As I watched these fellows two thoughts entered my mind. "There must be a better way of doing this" and "Why did I ever take that last pass to Philly when they were practicing rope descents?"

The rolling sea slowed up the unloading. When the sun set at 11:15 p.m., I was still sitting on the deck anxiously awaiting my turn. It came two hours later and it was pitch dark. As I climbed over the rail there weren't any doubts, those were big butterflies in my stomach. The equipment I was carrying didn't help. The big gas mask bag hung under my right shoulder while my full canteen was banging my left hip. A Carbine was strapped across my back over the back pack which contained half a tent, a raincoat, mess kit and two Army blankets. It was good to know that right before we jumped we were allowed to throw our packs into the boat. The fellow below me threw his and he hit nothing but water. I was hoping that my timing would be better. Never had I tried floating with a rifle around my head.

There was now a lot of shouting and cussing going on below me. The problem was some of the fellows were not jumping on command. I soon found out the reason for their hesitation. When I looked back over my shoulder all I could see, through the beams of three waving flashights, was water. This was a fine mess for a floater. Depending on the roll of the waves, the drop from the freighter was three to six feet. Twice the landing craft rolled into the freighter before the guy below me jumped. I was glad he didn't jump right away because it gave me a little visual timing practice before I would hear my "Now!"

The big voice boomed! I jumped and experienced great relief as I hit the deck wrapped in the arms of an unknown bruiser. I was quickly shoved to the front and joined a rank of buddies squeezed in like rows of sardines. As I glanced up at that freighter I emitted a victory sigh of relief.

We were crammed in rows six across. It was so dark all I could see were the helmets of the two fellows in front of me. Just seconds after we got underway the pilot swore a blue streak and threw the craft into reverse. We just barely missed another boat crossing our bow. The channel was full of these little LCs zigging and zagging from ship to shore. Our objective was a little, shrouded, green light sitting on the top of a ten foot pole stuck in the sand on Omaha beach.

When the boat nudged the beach everyone tumbled foward amid sighs of relief. The front of the LC was lowered and I quickly stepped off into knee deep, cold water. It was a stride that brought quick relief. Once again my feet were on terra firma.

The whiteness of the sand produced just enough light for us to observe that Omaha beach was jammed with silent soldiers. The thirty from our boat milled around our Sgt. and listened intently as he told us, "Get in single file, we are marching up and out of here and I want complete silence." The hard beach soon turned into soft sand. My mind flashed back to the good old days of running through the hot sand on the Jersey vacation beaches. As soon as we hit the hill we started to slip and slid and bump one another. Except for our huffing and puffing we staggered upward in utter silence. It was a new eerie experience being in a foreign country, in complete darkness, with the distant roll of the artillery making a new imprint on our expanding memories.

Fifteen minutes later we turned into a small field. We gathered around the Sgt. and he passed one short order:

"Quietly, find yourself an empty foxhole and get some sleep."

No-one needed any coaxing; to us rookies those war echoes had to be coming from the next field. A foxhole sounded like a great idea. I quickly found an empty one only to discover the nice guy that dug it was a midget. My calves and feet were pointed skyward. No matter, I snuggled in for a few hours of needed catnaps and I thanked the little guy for his efforts.

In the morning a typical Normandy haze greeted us. It was a surprise to find that most of our 783rd Company was in this square hedgerow field. As we crawled out of our holes and started to gather we were immediately warned to seperate ourselves. It was hard for us to realize that we were only a short distance from the front lines. It just seemed too calm for a war zone.

After a questionable breakfast consisting of a very dry prune bar, a small can of cold scrambled eggs and something that passed for coffee, Doggett, Wolf and I joined our drivers hiking to the beach to retrieve our trucks. It was a shocking sight. You could see there were blasted ships, tanks and trucks protruding from the lapping waves. It appeared that more men and equipment were blown up than ever reached the safety of the shore. We had not seen nor heard much news in the past week; now we didn't need to. As we drove off the beach, there was no question our troops took heavy casualties. We soon learned that, after eighteen days of heavy fighting, our best advance was just seven miles in from the channel.

By midafternoon the whole Company was assembled and we moved out in convoy. Driving parallel to the beach we quickly arrived in the headlined town of Carentan. We were enjoying our first ride in France not realizing that the front was just two miles to our left. Everything was very peaceful as we drove into St. Mere Eglise ten miles down the road. Moving around the vacant town square I looked up and I was thrilled to point out the church steeple from which John Steele, the Paratrooper, had hung playing dead until the battle was over. A few miles out of town we made our first camp right on the outskirts of Briqueville.

This whole area was apple orchard country. It took two normal size orchards to hide us and our trucks. The apple orchards were mostly square with hedgerow fences. This was not your ordinary American hedge. These hedgerows consisted of a solid dirt mound approximately five feet high. The mounds were covered with heavy gnarled bushes so thick it was impossible to walk or see through them. The orchards ranged in size from a half to two acres. Our trucks were quickly placed around the perimeters of the fields, under the trees and camouflaged. Our next order was, "Find yourself a nice safe spot and start digging." I dug mine long and deep. As for the apples, they were small and wormy causing farm boy Wolf to put it another way,

"These are the worst damn apples I have ever seen."

Some of the fellows dug two foxholes. The very first order of business was to place guard posts on the four corners of our area plus one at the Company gate. The guard posts always had the best foxholes. Having already learned the sound of "incoming mail," that of the dreaded 88 howitzer with its unique whistling wail, I needed no urging to dig my foxhole deep.

All the truck drivers were issued maps of the area so detailed they included tombstones in graveyards. I studied the map and it was plain to see why the 101st Paratroopers had only gained a couple hundred yards since D Day. For miles all of the land in front of us was a series of swamps. As the 83rd Division was now relieving the 101st Paratroopers, I didn't want to imagine what it was going to take to get the dug in Germans out of this no man's land.

For being just about two miles from the swamps our area was relatively quiet. During the day machine gun fire was plainly heard, but at night the Germans liked to play 4th of

July. Just about every night, around midnight, they would spray the area with 88s. For me it was perfect training for keeping one eye and one ear open.

A few days later they told us we could write home but there would be strict restrictions with censorship. Simply put, we could write about the weather in a positive way. No towns or any locations would be allowed, nor any type of fighting details or mention of equipment seen or used. Such items made razor cutting time for Lt. Gilman. Our immediate officer was also our private censor. These restrictions made good letter writing a chore. To remove some of the concern from the folks at home I wrote about the light side of Army life. This pleased everyone but Lt. Gilman whose most common sentence to me was,

"Rangnow, you're not writing again?"

****

Chapter 12

Normandy

Somewhere in France
June 26, 1944
"Well, do you still remember me? It has been a little while but let me assure you that all has been well in girly France. As for my quick exit from England — I was told my bad tennis was affecting the American morale.

Is your dear brother Chis over here? I'll be looking for him. I just hope he hasn't gotten so French that he greets me with a kiss.

As you have probably seen in the news reels, these French are overjoyed at seeing us. At times they seem overcome by it all. They just stand and stare at all our traffic jamming their small roads. I passed through one town today and, after seeing its destruction, I just sat and stared too.

The kids are the real fun. I've tried talking to them using my French handbook. Believe me I don't get very far before we all end up laughing. Their melodic chatter reminds me of how your going to sound in your sleep!

For sure I can't write home about the food. We're eating the boxed 10 in 1 rations. For a short spell some of the dishes are not too bad, but our boxes got all messed up and we keep getting the same menu. In writing Mom I said:

'If I ever complain about Tuesday leftovers just remind me of Army rations.'

As for our 'home', the Boy Scouts would love it. For sure it's not as hot as Tennessee but it's a lot drier. Washing out of your helmet is a revelation but it does save on water. I also think it's our secret weapon. In just a little while we'll be stinking out all the Germans.

Last night I got the good surprise of receiving your V Mail letter of June 13th. As for my needs? Please don't spend a lot of money. Any little package of cookies and candy will do."

****

June 29, 1944

In spite of all the evidence around it's still hard for me to realize that I'm actually in this war zone. I'm writing from my truck and I'm surrounded by bullet scarred trees. A few yards in front of me there's every kind of battered U.S. and German equipment that you can imagine. And, here's an odd fact of life for you. If I walk back just a few fields, the French are still living in their battered homes.

I'm sure you're worried about all the shooting, but the Germans rarely fire during the day. Our little scout planes simply zero in on their locations. At night we do hear the artillery but they are not firing at us."

(Of course, I was lying. The eerie sounds of the 88 gave everyone goose bumps. Their guns were close enough to hear them fire. Everyone became an expert at judging sound. If you could hear the whine, you knew the shell would land to either side of you. It was when you heard the firing but not the whine that you sweated it out until the shell exploded nearby.)

"As for the Air Force, they are doing a great job. We have yet to see an enemy plane. It will please you to know that my sleeping quarters are the best around. My foxhole is hip deep and its fully lined with cardboard. The bottom is very flat and level with two blankets serving as a mattress. The foxhole is covered by a full pup tent. Actually I sleep in the tent on a blanket alongside the foxhole. If the Germans get too disturbing, I retreat to the quiet of my hole."

(We are sleeping in the foxholes most nights because we're taking harassing fire every night. Last night they got a direct hit on our mess tent! So far we have been lucky but they are doing a good job of keeping us awake every night. I think I'm used to it now. I just roll into my hole and try not to dream of sleeping with my brother.)

June 30, 1944

"Well, this is a fine thing! You're now working full time at the NAVY DEPOT!! and you have been voted, 'The girl who is the most fun to be with.' Doesn't the Navy know there is a war going on? I'd like the names, ranks and ages of all these fellows. I assume you didn't get any girls votes. Now let me counter attack. A cute French girl just came up to me under this old apple tree and asked me for some, 'Sugh ra la.' I thought she wanted some sugar but it was candy. I couldn't resist her dimples so I gave her my last roll of Charms. She twinkled her eyes and said a sweet, English, 'Thank you.' The sad part of the story — she's just ten.

You might think an apple orchard would make a good camp ground. Actually it is a war hazard, not because Wolf keeps throwing apples at me, but because of the bees. You have to eat fast or you only get a half a ration. Somebody is getting bit every day but so far my aroma has held off the wrath of the French sting.

Worse than the bees are the dead cows. These huge, stinking cows are everywhere, laying on their backs, legs sticking straight up. The putrid odor permeates the air and sticks to the roof of your mouth. Long days have been spent digging holes and then trying to drag them in using the hoists on our trucks. Instead of seasick it's now cowsick. The cattle have been dead three weeks and it's tough learning how to pull them. Tying a chain around the bulls horns seemed like a logical answer but the horns pulled out with a sickening "Pop." Grabbing them by the legs produced the same result. The only solution was a grimy one. We rolled them over on the tow cable and dragged them to the nearest hole. All of us hate this 'cow detail' but we are almost gladly working our butts off just to get rid of this horrible ordor. These bees are smarter than we think. All they smell is sweet nectar."

****

Charlie Rohrer and I got out our maps today, hopped in a Jeep and went to the front for the first time. Some mortars needed repairing. One day at the front and my back hurts from walking around in a crouch. It was an interesting and humbling experience. Our infantrymen are dug in like pack rats. Sitting there, working on their mortars, Charlie and I looked like white Prince Charmings. I can't imagine how you keep your sanity living like they do.

Walking back out to pick up our Jeep we saw a field where the 101st Airborne gliders landed on June 5th. Every twenty feet the field had been staked out with tree poles to discourage any such landings. The poles sure did their job. Of the ten gliders that were in the field only two made a safe landing. The others looked like crushed match boxes. We walked over and I took some movies. Charlie took one look inside and said, " Can you imagine this night of horror, their war was over before they ever set one foot in France." Walking away, Charlie just missed triggering a wired mine strung along a little fence. After we both swallowed hard I joked, "Well, Charlie, at least we've had a couple of days in France."

Tonight we were told we have offically replaced the 101st on the front. Our war is about to begin.

****

Except for the fireworks, this 4th of July was unlike any I had ever seen. I was the guard at the hedgerow, main gate. We had been alerted to look for German paratroopers jumping in G.I. uniforms and speaking English. They told me to keep a check on the big field across from our main gate. At 4 a.m. I crossed the road and climbed over the hedgerow to take a look. Just as I knelt down, looking into the black darkness of this empty field, all hell broke loose. The whole sky flashed in flame. I dropped to the ground in a prone position feeling the earth shake under me. For an instant I was dumbfounded. No one told me the next field had a battery of eight inch guns. They, along with all our artillery, had fired together. After this initial shock I became engrossed by the sights and sounds of the continued firing. My fascination turned to alarm as I spotted a glimpse of someone crouching and moving across the far end of the field. Lightning thoughts flashed through my mind, "Why me, Lord?" It couldn't be, but I wasn't blind; I pleaded for another long round to let me see. Fire they did but I didn't see anyone. Nevertheless I backed into the corner of the hedgerow. There was another flash; this time there was no doubt. I spotted something moving in the opposite corner. The flashes were too fast for a good look. As I waited again the hair stood up on the back of my neck; now I HEARD movement coming toward me. Quickly, I went back to the prone position and aimed at the unknown. It seemed an eternity before they fired again. The field lit up again and running hard toward me were two horses. I let out a laugh of relief. I'm sure the horses were more scared than me.

Dear Ginny,

"Your mail is coming through in eight days. The first Stars and Stripes came out today and it says it is printed in France. It's only one page but it will bring us up to date with the news.

Our meals aren't as bad as the enclosed menu suggests. This is one of five menus so they are not boring, yet. Now Lt. Gilman is; he hand feeds us a cod liver oil pill after every dinner.

All kinds of surprises; your brother is still in England and Brog is going home. I never realized he was near 51 missions. He can't believe he's going home already. We'll wait and see but he sure deserves a good rest."

****

Like a lightning bolt the reality of war hit us today. We were eating noontime chow, separated and in small groups for safety, when a shot rang out. I grabbed my rifle and rolled over searching the hedgerows for a hidden sniper. There was yelling and some confusion and then all was quiet. Junior Levis was dead.

This is really hard to believe. This is only our second day on line and the jolly good kid of the Company is dead. I've been thinking of all the good times we had as bunkmates in the States and how we used to talk of the future. This is so sudden and final we are in shocked disbelief.

At four o'clock I went back on guard at the gate. A few minutes later I stood staring as Gin Ricky passed through bearing Junior's tarp-covered body. I shall never forget the sight of his shoes protruding from the open tailgate and the remorse I felt. With tears in my eyes I stood and saluted him as the truck slowly disappeared down the dusty, farm road. William "Junior" Levis is gone but my good friend will never be forgotten.

The devastating shelling yesterday was our curtain raiser. After two hours the shelling stopped and our infantry shoved off. The fighting through the hedgerows was deadly. All along the line many of our Divisions were engaged. Less than a thousand yards were gained. This war is far from over.

Right now Gene Bond and I don't have much instrument work so we are being kept busy by helping the rifle guys fix the damaged rifles coming from the front.

These smart Germans have been infiltrating our lines. They're stretching piano wire across the hedgerows and, because of dusty roads, our vehicles travel with the wind-shields laying down. This has resulted in a number of beheaded soldiers. Doc Pfeifer's automotive crew has been working dawn to dusk. Somehow they secured truckloads of angle iron. They cut it to size and weld it to the fronts of Jeeps making a foolproof wire cutter.

This morning Wolf and I drove back to the beach to pick up some supplies. As we passed through Carentan, we passed by an iron fenced school yard. It was crammed with standing GIs. This seemed strange but as we drew close no explanation was needed. These soldiers were all staring into space with a blank look. These poor guys were shell shocked troops waiting transportation back to England. Wolf turned to me and spoke first.

"Rags, you know what? War is hell."

****

"This is Sunday, July 9th. I'm writing from my cozy foxhole laying flat on my belly. It's warmer down here. After raining all day the sun just broke through at 10p.m. I'm also trying to catch this mouse that runs across my chest in the middle of the night. For two days I've been plugging up his hole but he digs another one. Maybe I'll leave him behind, rumors have us moving. It won't be far."

****

The next day we moved outside of St Mere Eglise behind another hedgerow but no apples. This has put us within three miles of our fighting buddies, and fighting they are. The 331st gained a thousand yards while the 329th and 330th repelled strong counter attacks from the 17 Panzer Division. For days the weather has been sour with no planes in the air. Since the 4th of July our advance has been held to 4,000 yards. It's hard to figure out how the Germans can be fighting on three different fronts and still be so strong along this front. Any thoughts of walking right through these guys have been set aside.

The weather has broken and on this 13th day of July Charlie Rohrer and I did an Army unthinkable—we volunteered! Lt. Gilman told us our mission was to go to the front and find discarded rifles left on the battlefield. Hearing the mission I turned to Charlie and said,

"Stan, now look what you got us into." He picked up the Hardy character and replied, "Ollie, it will be interestting. Maybe we'll find a Luger." Charlie is a gun nut.

After carefully studying the maps we drove the Jeep two miles and then slowly hoofed it. Jumping a hedgerow we saw M1s laying around. This seemed easy enough but, as we stacked the rifles, we discovered they were all splattered with blood and flesh. Rifle and German Burp gun firing seemed much too close for comfort. Crossing a little road we slowly looked at everything within sight and hearing. I took a flying broad jump over the next hedgerow and much to my horror, by one inch, my heels cleared the head of a dead American. Here were ten bloated bodies that looked more like big, purple Japs. I checked one of the fellow's dog tags. He was from Ohio. A thought crossed my mind. "I guess his parents know he has died but I'm sure glad they don't know he's been laying here since early July."

Directly in front of us there was a German hut. Again we slowly approached it and soon found an equal number of dead Germans. The smell in this field was worse than the dead cows. Inside the hut the table was set with real dishes that still contained their supper. It prompted me to remark, "Charlie, here's another version of the last supper." We had lost any thoughts of looking for Lugers. After removing all the rifles, from around and under the bodies, we made a hasty retreat for our deluxe camp.

It puzzled us why we were picking up and repairing all these damaged rifles. Our outfits were bringing them to us by the truck loads. To bat them out, Sgt. Harris organized a little production line. With Wolf we took a truck load of the fixed rifles back to a field near the Channel and we found our answer. Here was a whole line of soldiers taking target practice. After a few minutes of watching, Wolf and I looked at each other in amazement. These guys were raw rookies who were the replacements for our mounting casualties. We could not imagine that we were this short on replacements. Wolf summed it up quickly, "You know what, Rags? Our dream of getting to Berlin by Christmas now seems further away."

On returning I learned the prisoner I guarded in Camp Atterbury had shot himself in the foot. He said he was cleaning his rifle but he had been quoted, "I'll never go into combat." The Lt. thinks he's in for a rude awakening back in England. (He was court marshalled and served time.)

July15, 1944

"Here is a quick early morning epistle. Our long hours have made it tough to write so I want you to know that everything is A-OK. The rest of the world we don't know about. Haven't seen a Stars and Stripes in four days. We've heard the Russians are 100 miles from Germany. If that's true, they must think we're Boy Scouts.

You would enjoy the new fads breaking out. Some of the fellows have shaved heads while others are coming up with funny looking goatees. The Automotive section has put their talents together and they have a great hobby. I'm not telling our Dear Censor something he doesn't already know. They have assembled bits of tubing, jars and cans. In the can, over the fire, they have thrown in fruit cocktail and sugar. I haven't tasted any of it and by the looks on their faces, I won't be tempted."

****

Probably our greatest fear of the war was that of being gassed. All of us had seen the horror movies of World War I. When it came to gas mask training we all sat up and listened. We treated our new, "safe" gas masks as gently as our rifles. We expected the heartless Germans to use gas as soon as they got their backs to the wall. The Germans had to be thinking the same way because every captured German carried a gas mask.

Then a funny thing happened. Two weeks after landing, slowly but surely, gas masks were being left in tents or on the seats of trucks. Lt. Norton ranted and shouted and we all carried them again, but not for long. The word soon got back from the front that the infantrymen simply refused to carry the bulky extra bags. Before long the fear of gas was no longer an issue. Now they are history.

Today we moved for the third time. It was only two and a half miles but at least it's in the right direction. The digging of new latrines, garbage pits and foxholes is what gives us the appetite for another K ration.

July 16, 1944

"Here's some good news for you. We saw our first enemy plane today. Glancing up at them we thought they were ours. We felt a little dumb when the Ack Ack guns opened fire. They were shot down on the first pass.

Our treat tonight was real orange juice and a good mail call. I received a nice sweater and a mirror which groans every time I look into it. Eight Philadelphia Bulletins also arrived. They are fun to read but they are too optimistic. Printing that we'll be home by Christmas is just a bunch of hogwash."

****

Our camp is just west of St.Lo and very close to our front lines. There's another alert out for paratroopers and snipers. The first night in any new area can cause the guard posts to be a little jittery. Last night that is exactly what happened.

The area on the perimeter had been armed with our tin can alarm system. Tin cans were strung on string from tree to tree. Reinsburger and Kemper were on the midnight shift when they heard the cans rattle. Kemper tried to calm down Reinsburger by telling him it was probably just a rabbit. To calm his fears Kemper crawled out to double check. What caused the next event will never be known. When Kemper didn't find anything he got up and started back to his post. As he came into view Reinsburger shot him dead. To say the least, we are dumbfounded and angry. After all that training we're wondering, how do you prevent this type of tragedy? Our morale has taken a plunge. I don't know too much about Martin Kemper. He joined us right before we left the States and he wasn't in our Armament section. To me he was a very friendly and warm human being. He certainly didn't deserve to die like this. One also has to feel sorry for Reinsburger. His was a human mistake which he will carry for the rest of his life.

(Forty-seven years later Martin Kemper's cousin, Garth Kemper, contacted me from Virginia. He was only five when his Uncle was shot but, in an emotional plea, he wanted to learn all the details of his Uncle's service life. He also wrote that after the war they received a letter that had to be a most difficult letter to write. It was a remorseful letter to the family from Reinsberger.)

The following day Ginny informed me that she still didn't know we were in France. Puzzled I wrote back, "I don't understand. Two weeks ago we heard the German radio announce, 'The crack 83rd Div. is now in France.' But please don't believe everything you hear. Two days later they announced that we had been wiped out! Leave it to the Lt. and me, we'll tell you the truth. He just asked if I was writing another book for him to censor. 'Sir,' I said, 'You do have a heck of a job but look at it this way. Your getting some orginal one liners to use on your wife Pat.'

Ginny, have you read where they are now fining us two dollars if we're caught without a helmet or for not saluting an officer. I've got no problem with the helmet but, if I saluted Lt. Gilman every time we passed, he'd have one sore arm. Right, Sir?"

****

The Germans have given us another problem. They have this "Burp" gun which looks like a cheap tin toy. It's very light and small but it emits a short, scary burp of bullets. To counteract this advantage we are making a few changes in our Carbine which makes it an automatic. Again, George Harris has pressed everyone he can get to form another production line. It's surprising, we are on double daylight saving time which truly allows us to work until the midnight sun goes down. This week we have batted out 300 Carbines making the Infantry guys very happy.

On this July 22nd we are in good spirits. Radio reports have the Russians 50 miles from Warsaw. With the news of Hitler's assassination plot, plus all the other unrest in Germany, we almost had a mild celebration. We've heard reports that, "Stalin is giving Germany 72 hours to surrender and that revolution has broken out in Germany. Some of the guys are making bets that the war will be over in three days! I'll play, wait and see.

July 22, 1944

Now, Ginny, I'm going to relate a story of last night just to
prove to you we do have some fun. Muss Musser and I had
the evening off so we started walking back toward jolly
England. After a mile or so we came to some farmers
pitching hay. We watched and they smiled until they somehow got us pitching the hay. Communicating was done with
gestures, plus some 'Wee's.' They motioned for us to follow
them back to the farmhouse. What a surprise! Here was a
huge dinner table all set up and women of all ages scurrying
around. French wasn't needed to realize they wanted us to
share their meal. Of course we already had chow so how do
you say "No Merci," without hurting international relation-
ships?

Before we had a chance to think they stuck a big glass of
wine in our hands. For some reason I whispered to Muss,

'Don't drink too fast or they'll fill it up again.'

The meal itself isn't something I'm writing home about
but it sure came from the heart. There were bowls and bowls
of steaming potatoes plus large bowls of hot red beets.
What's a French meal without baskets of French bread?
There were also two small platters of divine meat. With a
pantomime of hands and lips we succeeded in getting across
that we would not eat their scarce meat. They laughed,
waved their arms and filled our glasses again.

After a dessert of unsweetened pastry the table was cleared.
Vin and I were bloated. No matter, the music and dancing
began. EVERYONE wanted to dance with the two left
footed Americans. This included six-year-old girls,
grandmothers and the nice inbetween ones!! Their style of
dancing sure wasn't Glenn Miller. By the fourth dance our
tongues were hanging out. With questioning eyes, Muss and
I looked at one another asking, 'How are we going to get out

of this?' Seeing the sweat on our brows our hosts let us sit down but gave us new smaller glasses. With the glasses came the hard stuff and a dumb French custom. All the girls insisted on taking turns sitting on our laps. The men laughed. Muss is far from tall, and with the big grandmoms on his lap, all we could see were his shoes.

Two hours later I was concerned. How much more of this would my stomach take? There also was a long hike, before dark, facing us. Gradually we succeeded in making an exit. Then arm in arm we stumbled through the darkening fields taking turns throwing up. This morning we agreed, it was a night not to be forgotten — nor repeated."

****

It's six weeks into battle. We're concerned because we or the British haven't broken through anywhere. The bad weather this week has grounded our needed air power.

The artillery was now in need of daily maintenance. Our team was headed up by Staff Sgt. Earl "Baldy" Graham. He had one mechanic and an instrument man. Gene Bond gave me a choice. I could go with the daily team or we could take turns working in the truck. I told him I'd gladly do the daily front line routine. The conditions are a challenge.

As needed I'll assist Graham, but my job will be to check the telescopic scopes on the howitzers. These humid days and the cool nights are causing moisture problems. The lens has to be removed and the inside dried. Damaged scopes are replaced and returned to Doggett's instrument truck. Besides its work benches, tools and supplies, the truck is a bright, warm, meeting place at night.

Working with Harris and Graham is a real pleasure. Both are in their mid thirties and they present kind of a fatherly figure. Rank doesn't mean much. Bond is six years my senior from Lansing, Michigan. He is a dependable friend. As long as we do our work we are all treated as equals and, if it wasn't for the shelling, the weather and the chow, we could almost be having a good time.

July 24, 1944

"Sitting against this old apple tree you wouldn't believe the spectacular air show. First there were hundreds of P-47s flying in long strings. A little later came the drone of the Flying Fortresses. They were flying in squadrons of twelve and they kept coming for over an hour. It's an awesome sight and it appears they are attempting to knock the Germans out of the swamp. Not only can we plainly hear the explosions, we can feel them."

July 25, 1944

"After guard duty last night I had sleep-in privileges this morning. The sounds of 'droning bees' awoke me. As I came crawling out I got a real eye opener. In every direction, as far as you could see, the sky was full of every type of fighter and bomber. The planes just kept coming in wave after wave. It made yesterday's raid seem small. There was no question they were hitting the swamps again.

Half an hour later we were surrounded in confusion. A sudden fog rolled in over the area but the sun was out. The ground was trembling. The thick dust started everyone coughing. We didn't know which way to go. The bombing had caused a huge dust storm. Fortunately a breeze came up and blew most of it away."

There were over 2,500 bombers in that raid. They wiped out the target markers thus causing many casualties within the front line troops, including General Roosevelt. The bombing has raised our morale sky high. Our infantry has started to move through the swamps. This looks like the start of the "big push."

After we finished our work on some howitzers Graham, Wolf and I drove to the outskirts of St.Lo. This bombing by the Air Force has leveled the whole town to the point that all one can see is just a few walls and chimneys. It is an unbelievable sight. It had to be a nightmare for anyone still living there.

On the lighter side, I think when our troops return home there will be a sexual revolution. These French women are so seductive our poor guys have learned all kinds of new approaches. It's very common for women, of all ages, to come to a guard post with all kinds of suggestions. It's so bad, that for candy bars or a few cigarettes, these free spirited gals will invite you into the nearest bush.

Two fellows, who will go unnamed, told us of their adventurous evening. Mom invited them home to spend the night with her and her daughter. The Mom had quite a sense of humor. She tied little bells to the coil spring of her daughter's bed.

The native men are also uninhibited. Doggett and I were driving down this main road where we met the usual sight of a farmer and his wife hauling hay. On passing everyone waves, but this fellow had to be different. He handed the horse's reins to his wife. Then waving at us with one hand he peed with the other.

Joe Neff, from Burholme, found me today to tell me that Calvin Randolph, of Crescentville, had been killed. They are both in our 308 Medics. Old Cal and I sat side by side through our last six years of school. Joe's news brought back many good high school memories. Once again, I realized I had drawn the long straw.

****

Chapter 13

The Breakthrough

July 29, 1944

"Ginsy, here's a short but sweet one. The past two days and nights have been very busy for us. The news on the two fronts, that's Russian, has us in high spirits.

Again, I can't tell you where we are, but by the time you read this I hope we're in Paris!

The enclosed is one of the cute leaflets that we are dropping on Jerry. Take it over to my Pop and he will decipher it."

****

After being cooped up on the Normandy beachhead for a month it was hard to realize the armies had broken out so fast and so far. We were now sixty miles in from the beach. Passing through the towns of Granville and Avarnches reminded me of back to back 4th of July parades. All the streets were jammed with waving and cheering people. The great thing was the Germans were running so fast the towns didn't suffer a scratch. I have never seen everyone's spirits so high. For sure we're on our way to Paris, but the target is still Berlin.

Sunday, August 7, 1944

"Sorry about the writing gap. It's been very difficult staying up with all these fast moving events, 'U.S. Troops in Brest and Paris.' I also can't believe the Philadelphia news. How can Americans go on strike just because they hired blacks to run the trolleys? Is it true they have soldiers riding guard in every car? That is upsetting!

The solution is simple. Get the Union leaders over here and stick them on the front lines for a couple of days and some common sense might return. While I'm still mad, I think I'll write a letter to the editor. So what if I do blow my home coming parade!

Doggett is a great friend. He's driving me through this little town and he spots a pretty girl waving a glass. This is too much for old Art. He came to a sliding halt and, presto, we're drinking cider with her. Within a minute all the neighbors had our Jeep surrounded and they were slapping our backs and pumping our hands. It's tough driving these roads. Our arms get so tired waving we're now taking ten minute turns. However, if your not waving, you can't just relax; you must maintain a frozen grin.

This life is completely different from Normandy. It's good to see so many happy people getting back to leading normal lives. The front has moved so fast we no longer hear the artillery."

****

Jerry is cornered against the sea in Brest and St. Malo. The German Army is in a shambles. There's no question this whole section will be ours in a short time. Maybe a complete victory isn't so far off after all.

On August 11th Wolf was driving me and Tech./ Sgt.Litrenta, back to a depot with damaged equipment. Now Litrenta is okay, but he's from South Philadelphia, which could be the reason for his loud, bossy manner. I was just settling myself amongst the equipment when Wolf swerved the Jeep. A rifle went bouncing on the road. Litrenta ran back to pick it up but, when he stooped, a bullet whistled by his rump. Never have we seen Bill run so fast. Rumors that snipers were in the woods were no longer a rumor. (And, that was the last time the Sgt. ever set foot out of a front line camp.)

When I returned I went right on guard duty. This time the guard posts were located 400 yards outside the camp. There are four men to a post. We were dug in with shallow foxholes. At night two men were to stay awake, but I didn't think this was necessary as we were sleeping within arms reach of each other. A vote was taken and Mel Schlottman was the lone dissenter. Finally we convinced him. Not only would we get two more hours of sleep but no Officer, or the Sgt. of the Guard, would venture to our post in darkness.

Mel was rewarded with the first shift at midnight. I had just dozed off when Mel yanked my foot. In his Pennsylvania Dutch accent Mel declared, "Dares something crawling out dare." All of us quickly rolled over into the prone position straining our eyes and ears into the darkness. After a few, long minutes we all agreed Mel had heard a rabbit.

Two more times Mel awakened us blowing our idea for getting sleep. Suddenly a loud rustling was heard! The morning's sniper popped into my mind. There had to be six Jerries crawling toward us. The noise was stopping and starting but coming right toward us. Rolling over to Woody I said, "On the count of three, throw a hand grenade to your right." We both threw and all became quiet on the Western Front.

At the crack of dawn we went out to find all the dead bodies. There wasn't even the trace of a rabbit tail. This was going to be embarrassing. I asked everybody to retreat back to the post while I tried to sneak up. I walked and I crawled but, everytime their answer was always the same,

"You sound like a Sherman tank!" A short time later Lt. Brown came out to inquire about the grenades. He simply laughed then added, "Well, you all learned something from the experience and you did the right thing."

August 15, 1944

"Do you hear all that chatter? That's a dozen women and kids, no men. We put up all kinds of 'Off Limit' signs but the women just keep coming through the bushes. Last night I was trying to take a helmet bath and I ended up sprinting for a large fig leaf."

Our 83rd Infantry is engaged in house to house fighting cleaning out the towns of Dinard and St.Malo. The German's backs are against the sea and we've been taking hundreds of Jerries a day. One oddity is the Division is being shelled by German naval guns implanted on the little island of DeCezembre about three miles off the coast.

****

August 15, 1944

"Sooner or later I knew you would ask my opinion on the French girls. Of course, we are faced with the fact that after you haven't seen the opposite sex for awhile they're all going to look a lot better! Some of these girls have freaky hair styles with weird colors. Try purple or an ugly orange. Somehow, unlike the British, these girls have lipstick and silk stockings. If we get to Paris, I'll work up a scientific report.

Corporal Lester Wolf
The Ohio farm boy who became—"Best Friend" to many.

The barracks at Camp Atterbury.

The "neat" mess hall.

First Sergeant
"Big Jim" jones

Lt. Knoerl

My barracks advisor, "Reds" Rennie.

Cooling The Feet—25 Mile Hike
"Old Dog", Rags, and Bond.

My sketch of nurse—"Cute Stuff".

Barracks at Aberdeen, Maryland
Nicknamed "Skunk Hollow" because of soft coal smoke.

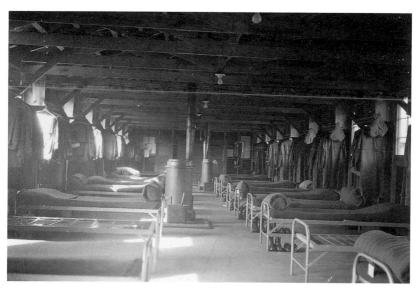

"Plush"—Sleeping quarters.

Rags and Ginny—April 1943.

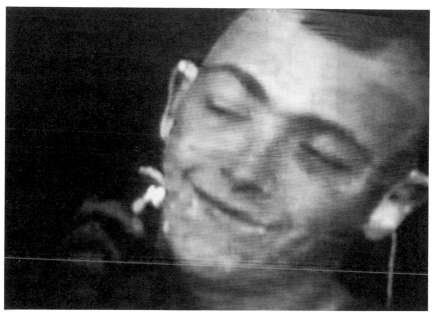

Pvt. William Levis—"Junior"
Behind the hedgerows Jr. was finishing up his mohawk haircut. This photo,
taken with a movie camera, was Jr.'s last. He was killed the next day.

SUPREME HEADQUARTERS
ALLIED EXPEDITIONARY FORCE

Soldiers, Sailors and Airmen of the Allied Expeditionary Force!

You are about to embark upon the Great Crusade, toward which we have striven these many months. The eyes of the world are upon you. The hopes and prayers of liberty-loving people everywhere march with you. In company with our brave Allies and brothers-in-arms on other Fronts, you will bring about the destruction of the German war machine, the elimination of Nazi tyranny over the oppressed peoples of Europe, and security for ourselves in a free world.

Your task will not be an easy one. Your enemy is well trained, well equipped and battle-hardened. He will fight savagely.

But this is the year 1944! Much has happened since the Nazi triumphs of 1940-41. The United Nations have inflicted upon the Germans great defeats, in open battle, man-to-man. Our air offensive has seriously reduced their strength in the air and their capacity to wage war on the ground. Our Home Fronts have given us an overwhelming superiority in weapons and munitions of war, and placed at our disposal great reserves of trained fighting men. The tide has turned! The free men of the world are marching together to Victory!

I have full confidence in your courage, devotion to duty and skill in battle. We will accept nothing less than full Victory!

Good Luck! And let us all beseech the blessing of Almighty God upon this great and noble undertaking.

Dwight Eisenhower

General "Ikes" letter was delivered to all front line troops.

MENU No. 3

FOR 5 COMPLETE RATIONS USE CON-
TENTS OF THIS BOX TOGETHER
WITH CANNED GOODS IN BOX
MARKED "2ND HALF OF 5 RATIONS"

★ ★

————BREAKFAST————

CEREAL   HAM AND EGGS
            BISCUITS AND JAM
            COFFEE AND MILK

————DINNER————

1 K RATION UNIT PER MAN
1 CAN K RATION
MEAT PER MAN

————SUPPER————

CORNED BEEF   PEAS
        BISCUITS AND BUTTER
FRUIT BAR   ORANGE DRINK
WHAT No PUMPKIN PIE!

HALAZONE TABLETS ARE INCLUDED
TO PURIFY WATER FOR DRINKING.
(SEE DIRECTIONS ON THE BOTTLE.)

LOOK FOR A CAN OPENER IN A
SMALL ENVELOPE IN THIS BOX

★ ★

One of the three C ration menus.

Passierschein

(GÜLTIG FÜR EINEN ODER MEHRERE ÜBERBRINGER)

Der deutsche Soldat, der diesen Passierschein vorzeigt, benutzt ihn als Zeichen seines ehrlichen Willens, sich zu ergeben. Er ist zu entwaffnen. Er muß gut behandelt werden. Er hat Anspruch auf Verpflegung und, wenn nötig, ärztliche Behandlung. Er wird so bald wie möglich aus der Gefahrenzone entfernt.

DWIGHT D. EISENHOWER
Oberbefehlshaber
der Alliierten Streitkräfte

Englische Übersetzung nachstehend. Sie dient als Anweisung an die alliierten Vorposten.

SAFE CONDUCT

(VALID FOR ONE OR SEVERAL BEARERS)

The German soldier who carries this safe conduct is using it as a sign of his genuine wish to give himself up. He is to be disarmed, to be well looked after, to receive food and medical attention as required, and to be removed from the danger zone as soon as possible.

DWIGHT D. EISENHOWER
Supreme Commander,
Allied Expeditionary Force

A German Pass dropped behind the Lines in Normandy.

1st Lt. Ivan Gilman. My boss and "Dear Censor."
This is a movie, TV photograph.

Our "Dear Censor," Lt. I. Gilman, insisted I was trying to harass him with the location of my artwork.

Open Air Repair Shop.
Vin Musser and Charlie Rohrer.

T/Sgt. George Harris—Armament Section leader.

Blasting the Germans out of the walled city of St. Malo.

Visiting the famous "Off Limits" Mont Saint-Michel.
L to R: Sgt. Litrenta, Les Wolf and Rags.

The "Have Nots" hoping for left-overs. Note shoes.

Lt. Kimball, "What the hell's going on here?"

The battle of The Bulge is over so the Red Cross Girls serve coffee.
L to R: Phillips, Rorther, MacMillan and Company Commander, Lt. Norton.

Our first class 40 by 8 to cross three countries.
Burns, Forster, Wolf, Smitty and Manning standing.

A rare German "Buzz" bomb. The pilot aimed and then jumped!
On exhibit, Rheims, France.

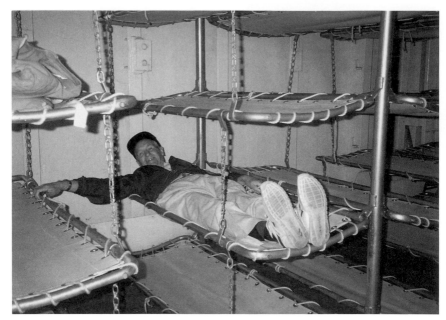

Sleeping position on the "Sea Ashe".
(A restored Liberty ship—1992)

Les Wolf's snowy farewell—Harrisburg station.

Please tell Rudolph his latest Rangnow wrapped package arrived in good shape. He also invented a new cookie which eliminates brushing. The darn top of the Dr. Lyons Tooth Powder can popped off.

With the sudden invasion of southern France I'm now ready to make General Sharpless another ice cream bet. The war will be over by October 15th!"

August 18, 1944

"Here is, I hope, the uncensored story of the day that Lt. Gilman promised us if we finished our work first. So I fixed nine instruments on five guns before noon. Then we made a detour from the front. We included Wolf, Rohrer and Litrenta. All I can say about where we went is, it's a very historical site. The big treat was our dinner. It was something out of hollywood, quaintly French with candlelight to boot.

Picture this! Four very dirty GIs sitting at a little round table covered with a spotless white tablecloth. Protruding from under the table were our helmets and rifles. When our blonde waitress came and rattled something in French, Wolf answered authoritatively, "Wee." This proper reply brought us sliced tomatoes, radishes and hard French bread. As we continued our excited chatter Blondie came back waving her arms at us. Can you imagine, she had to tell GIs to start eating fresh food?

When we finished she took both the plates and the silverware! In a flash there sitting before us was the biggest, fluffy, light omelet I have ever seen. After the dishes and silverware disappeared again Wolf asked, 'Is the dishwasher included in the price?'

Two great bottles of red wine were served along with the main course, which included tender cuts of roast pork and crispy, large french fries. The meal was properly finished with a light dessert of fresh apricots.

As we smacked our lips, I was handed the bill and I got the biggest surprise. I was the only one with money so I coughed up the $28.00. A French bargain for four."

****

The historic site was Mont St.Michel. For a bar of soap and three Mounds bars, a nice old lady gave us the guided, historical tour of the citadel island.

Today we moved to a central location just east of Dinan. It's so quiet there's not a foxhole to be found. Our supplies are short, which means C rations again. At least I can still taste the St.Michel feast.

Friday, September 1, 1944
"You can thank our Dear Lt.for your lack of mail. He sent us away for three days. Fortunately for him it was an interesting, censored trip.

Dog and I were on guard today at a post right next to a house. A grandmom just came out and gave us a bottle of wine and a bag of hazel nuts. Now where did she get those fresh nuts? War is crazy."

****

Our trip was to St.Malo. Because of the distance they wanted us to stay there. Our artillery was firing point blank at the island of DeCezembre. From a second floor apartment we watched low flying B24s dropping their "jelly" bombs. Within seconds the whole island was engulfed in soaring flames. Nobody could live through that or so we thought. The very next bomber got hit and it plunged into the sea and disappeared. It was a sad ending to an amazing show. More amazing is the fact that they have been bombed for two weeks and they're still firing back.

On Sept.2nd the Germans on the island waved the white flag just as I watched our infantry getting into landing craft. A surprising number of 323 men and women had survived all that bombing and shelling.

By Sept.9th the whole area was taken and we began tearing down all the howitzers in the Division. We worked all day long in heavy rain, but we slept well at night. The Division was catching its breath and working its way back up to full strength.

Thanks to captured German rations we are eating better. The mess Sgt. traded canned chicken, cherries and apple sauce for good French bread and potatoes. There are also some rather good German hot dogs, but I think eighteen crates stacked ten feet high is a little much.

This 16th day of September has made history for the 83rd Div. A Lt. Magill from the 331st Infantry, with just 12 men, somehow captured 20,000 Germans retreating from southern France at the Loire river. The German General, General Elster, wanted to stage a mock battle to save face but General Macon refused. I wrote Ginny, "Reporters have been all around the area so maybe now you'll learn where we are." The other amazing sight was seeing these endless columns of Germans marching across the river to surrender. Now we're working our butts off dispersing all these men, rifles, vehicles plus horses. The soldiers are corralled like a herd of cows in wired off fields.

After seeing this it's not hard to believe that victory could be around the next corner.

September 14, 1944

"Ginny, here's some more Army humor. All kinds of
German supplies have been falling into our hands. Somehow Lt. Norton got lucky enough to have his tent surrounded by stacked cases of wine. He then declared anyone
found around his tent at night would be shot. Someone (I can
now confess it was me) put a cartoon on the bulletin board
depicting the Lt., standing guard over his cases, with a black
Hitler mustache. Of course, the whole Company was looking and laughing. — So what happened? As evening chow
was called, Lt. Norton stood at the end of the line and gave
each of us a bottle of wine."

****

For the past two weeks I have been traveling with the
artillery team getting all the kinks out of the howitzers. It
looks like the 83rd is spread all over France. Our 83rd Recon
drove 200 miles down to Bordeaux and they didn't find one
German. While we were away the Company moved to
Chateaubriant and now we are just east of Orleans. That's
south of Paris. Everything seemed great until I read the
casualty figures for the first three weeks in Normandy. The
total was 60,771 of which 8,974 were killed.

We have been left far behind the front. All our armies are
again lined up, but this time it's on their German border.
One big push and this could be over. For sure this 83rd Div.
is prepared to fight again. The big question on everyone's
mind is, where are we going?

Lt. Gilman just informed me that I could tell Ginny we
were now in the Third Army. He then commented, "Send
Ginny my love." I did as ordered then added, "Ginny,
tonight you'll probably have a nightmare."

****

Chapter 14

Luxembourg

The next day, September 27, the whole Company rolled out in convoy, heading east. It proved to be an interesting, exhausting drive. The war had not touched this part of France. It seemed like we were riding back in time. In the smaller villages the farmhouses and yards were right on the roads. Manure piles were flowing their juices down the gutters causing many a "Phew." Wolf countered with, "Ah, haw, it's beginning to smell more like home."

The weather could have been better and our gas tanks should have been bigger. Our orders were to go as far as we could and that sure created a mess. Garrison was riding with me and we both thought, here we go again. The gas tank was on empty. We were passing gasless trucks. It was no longer a convoy. It was every man for himself. Gin Ricky gave her last gasp just as it was getting dark. We coasted into a wooded area to wait for the overworked gas-line fairy.

By luck we found a southern speaking outfit. They did not have any gas but by flashlight we accepted their hot chow. Returning for breakfast we discovered they were the Quartermaster truckers who just happened to be black! Two hours later we were gassed and on our way. Six of us found one another and formed our own convoy. Finally we found our leader who told us, "Follow me, we're headed for a new country, Luxembourg."

It poured all day long. At dusk we pulled into a valley outside the city and for the second, cold night we curled up on the front seat of Gin Ricky.

The next day at noon, with the Company in full convoy, we started our march through the city of Luxembourg. The city had only been freed three weeks ago. Everyone was in high spirits. It was an unbelievable reception. The second surprise was our new camp turned out to be a small school just blocks from the heart of this modern city.

****

In writing Ginny I couldn't tell her where I was, but I gave her plenty of clues to work on. "We are now sleeping on cots, which should help get that long trip out of our system. Musser and I had a nice stroll around town and we found it easy to talk to the people. Many spoke English. I had a hot shower in a nice tile bath on top of a large modern theatre showing, 'It Started With Eve.' Crazy war isn't it? This place is too good to be true. We're sure to move tomorrow."

It didn't take long to learn that the front and Germany were fifteen to thirty miles away. This is a small country just 175 miles long, but it was also surprising to learn the 83rd, plus some attached units, were the country's entire defense.

Our Infantry has been fighting house to house in Remick, the last, large town held by the Germans. Each morning three or four of us visit the artillery. This is pretty country. I wrote Ginny, "The ride to the front is on narrow, tree lined

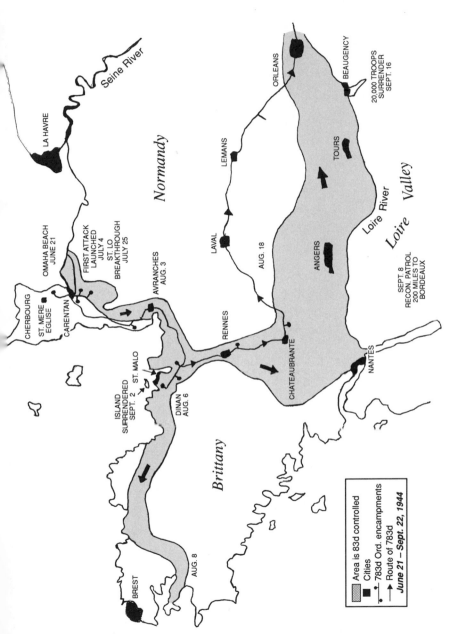

CHERBOURG

ST. MERE EGLISE

OMAHA BEACH
JUNE 21

CARENTAN

FIRST ATTACK
LAUNCHED
JULY 4

ST. LO
BREAKTHROUGH
JULY 25

AVRANCHES
AUG. 3

Seine River

LA HAVRE

Normandy

LEMANS

LAVAL

AUG. 18

ORLEANS

BEAUGENCY

20,000 TROOPS
SURRENDER
SEPT. 16

TOURS

ANGERS

Loire River

Loire Valley

SEPT. 8
RECON. PATROL
200 MILES TO
BORDEAUX

RENNES

CHATEAUBRANTE

NANTES

ISLAND
SURRENDERED
SEPT. 2   ST. MALO

DINAN
AUG. 6

Brittany

AUG. 8

BREST

Area is 83d controlled
Cities
783d Ord. encampments
Route of 783d
June 21 – Sept. 22, 1944

Invasion — June 6 to September 16, 1944

roads, running through well kept farms. However, the ground at the front is the muddiest mud any of us have known. Walking conditions are hazardous to one's welfare especially when we need the heavy tool box. Gin Ricky has been stuck so bad Wolf and I had to winch her out using trees as anchors. No-one is going anywhere on this front unless we get a good dry spell."

October 11, 1944

"I've told you about this modern city with its ice cream and pie but it's not all that great. The fence around our schoolyard is the typical, tall, black iron type. Our mess truck is in one corner of the yard and every day kids and old folks come and wait for us to finish eating. It's been a little gross. Normally we use our left over coffee to wash our mess kits into the garbage can. The kids were scooping this sloppy mess out and taking it home. Most of us then took all the food allowed, eating half of it and dumping the rest into the children's pails protruding through the fence.

The high command couldn't allow this to continue so today everything was moved from the fence. This solved our problem. The sad, hungry faces of the little ones are still there, staring.

On the lighter side Doggett is threatening to shoot the radio if he hears Bing Crosby sing these same two songs, AGAIN. They are, 'When The Lights Go On Again' and 'Long Ago And Far Away.' Songs can get depressing.

Ginny, the papers are overplaying these reports of the fighting man and the farmers daughters. Generally all they get to hug is the ground. Now, back here it is a different matter. We do have cigarettes and candy. Their husbands are either longtime prisoners or probably dead. It's very hard for me to judge people in a war. Bond is my problem. He thinks he's in love. We razz him but he continues to push this girl's baby carriage around town. Oh, Boy!"

****

"It's October 15, my predicted end of the war day. Don't laugh, this war is far from over. In spite of the worsening mud, our day at the front was different. When we arrived at the 155s they were firing at 3 o'clock. Receiving a cease fire allowed me to work on a gunsight for a minute. Then they received a call. The target was now 9 o'clock! Boy, this was a little unreal and difficult. It meant digging the gun out, turning it around, then digging it back in, in all this thick mud. If your Dad is scratching his head, that's okay. I'd tell you the answer but our Dear Lt. is poised with his razor."

The answer was simple. The gun was positioned in a bend of the river making it possible to fire on a 180 degree axis and hit Germany in both directions.

As we waited for the sunshine to dry up and stiffen the mud, both sides played the old cat and mouse game. Later in October our forces laid down a dense smoke screen along the Sauer river from Echternach to Palzen, a distance of 18 miles. This was followed by tremendous barrages from all our artillery and mortars. Generally this signalled an attack by the infantry but not this time. The Germans seemed confused. Their return fire was heavy, to slow, to none. Late in the afternoon the German radio announced, "In Luxembourg a strong enemy attack has been thrown back."

From thirty miles away, on October 30, they turned the tables on us by shelling the City of Luxembourg. My first thought was "Buzz Bombs," but there hadn't been any loud buzzing. The poor civilians thought the Germans had broken through. Two houses were being leveled with just one shell. The attack lasted for two hours. We were lucky they missed our schoolhouse by a block. Later we learned this mysterious shelling had been done by a single gun. Seventeen rounds had been fired from a huge 280mm railway gun.

The river was the border of the front line and, with the hilly countryside, it was possible for both sides to observe careless movement. Getting to some of the mortar positions became interesting. One day Musser, Rohrer and I had to park a mile away. Coming over the last hill we resorted to stooping and crawling. Suddenly all hell broke loose. Both sides were firing artillery over our heads. We laid down and waited out what sounded like a very busy freight yard.

While fixing the mortars one of the fellows suggested we should sneak down and peer around the corner of the last house, "To see a sight you have never seen!" Off the three of us went and, reaching the corner, Musser kneeled down and I peeked over his shoulder. Sure enough, there it was 200 yards away, the Moselle river. It looked like a creek. In plain view on the opposite bank were houses. There it was — GERMANY — so close and yet so far.

On the drive home we discussed the current state of affairs. The whole front was stuck in the mud, but freezing temperatures were close at hand. The next big push had to be to the north or south of us. We feared that the Germans might learn that we were the only Division guarding this little country. But once again we were rested and at full strength. It was a mutual feeling; our Luxembourg vacation was coming to an end.

It is now November 1st. As we walked up to the first howitzer we were greeted with gloom. Last night an 88 landed three feet from the 155 and killed one of the crew. He had become a good friend. The Colonel figured there was a spy in the village so he ordered that all the villages near the river had four hours to evacuate. That afternoon the road back to Luxembourg was not only jammed but it was the saddest of sights. People were acting as horses pulling their stacked carts of family possessions. Luckier ones had cows pulling wagons while almost everyone, including the very old, were struggling with back packs. The familiar daily waves and smiles were gone. War is hell.

The weather changed on November 6. "It snowed for the first time today, a relief from the rain. It didn't lay and, when six of us tried to find our way home from the movies, it was so dark we could not see our hand in front of our face. Wolf hit his shin on a parked Jeep and Musser fell over a step. We had quite a few blocks to walk with many turns. Out of the darkness Phillips said, 'When I was a boy and got in trouble I was told to look up.' There was a loud groan but he was right. By walking with our heads looking up we could make out the house tops. The rest was easy, but now my head is stuck up. Ho, Ho!

Our school home has been turned into a real school and the pupils are us. If these two hour sessions continue, Sir, we're going to demand college night credits."

****

On November 12th I was telling Ginny about three more days of rain. "The muddy roads drive like an icy road. You turn the wheel and nothing happens. Today our winch saved us three times. It sure feels good now to be sitting in a dry, warm room. But it's not all that good. Our German hot dogs got us in the end. Moaning from cramps are coming from everywhere and with 150 men using 8 toilets I can assure you that more than one man has broken the record for the fifty yard dash. A group with GIs is a funny, sad sight."

The first snow to lay came on November 14. I was writing Ginny and watching the city turn into a Christmas scene. Suddenly there was the sound of a passing freight train running right across the school roof. The windows were rattling violently, followed by instant silence and then a few seconds later a sizeable explosion erupted two blocks away. Luxembourg had been hit with its first Buzz bomb. These bombs were spine chilling because you could hear, as well as see, them coming. All you could do was hold your breath and hope the motor didn't stop. A second after the little, winged bomb lost power it dove straight into the ground.

November 21, 1944

"It was great getting your Christmas package but I disobeyed your, 'Do not open till Christmas.' The Army overruled you. Can you visualize us getting a move order and having everyone loaded down with packages? The wallet and gloves are already in use and your 'funny' toilet paper became a serious gift. Yes, the GIs struck again! Dog wants to thank you too, 'I like her style and brand.'

The Christmas packages have given us a lot to laugh about. Wolf got a package of tea bags. He hates tea! Earl Graham received three different size combs. He's bald! But a letter sent to one of the supply men took the cake. It was three years late, from the Government, informing him he was 4A and wouldn't be called.

Lt. Gilman was just here passing out cigars. Yes, a little weird. The occasion, he is now a First Louie! This afternoon we presented Ivan with his helmet. His new silver bar is one of a kind, measuring five eighths of an inch square by three inches long. Poor Ivan just shook his head and remarked, 'You guys are too much.'"

On Thanksgiving I wrote Ginny the full details of our special dinner. First the officers pulled guard for us and then the whole Company lined up and marched to a private cafe. The wide eyed civilians had never witnessed such a sight. Each soldier was carrying a knife, fork and spoon. It was a great, wine to mints, dinner but that didn't fool Wolf, "Ragsy, I smell a skunk. I think they're trying to tell us something."

How right he was. The next night the Company was divided in half. On offense one night and the next defense. We took to the woods with blackened faces and played the war games of Tennessee. However, this was a far cry from summer maneuvers. It was cold, muddy and a sure sign we were headed for Germany. Rumors have us relieving the 4th Div. which has had a fierce struggle fighting to get through the Hurtgen Forest outside Aachen. The whole front has been relatively quiet but the mud is getting hard. Everyone is well supplied and rested. It just seems logical that it's time to resume the race to Berlin.

Thursday, December 7, 1944

"Pearl Harbor Day. Boy, there's been so many changes since then, that day seems like ten years ago.

This quick, short letter is to tell you again not to worry. It means when you do get our mail it will be in bunches and by the time you read this you will understand it's always for military reasons."

Two hours later we were climbing through the evergreen mountains of Belgium. It started to snow and the forest was quickly transformed into a winter wonderland. Many hours later we came down the mountain to enter the untouched city of Verviers. Going in the opposite direction for a needed rest was the 4th Armored Division. Leaving the last line of buildings we approached a large meadow and, suddenly, there it was. A ribbon of miniature, concrete pyramids winding their way over hill and valley. It seemed impossible that anyone could have believed the Siegfried Line could stop an Army. The pyramids were covered with dirt. In seconds we were across to be greeted by the sign we longed to see, "Entering Germany."

If nothing else, the line created a time zone for suddenly the ravages of war were everywhere. As we drove through Aachen there was nothing but total destruction. Our convoy was snaking its way around rubble and bull dozers which were mopping up the main highway. It was a deserted city but it contained our new home, a bombed out German barracks whose last tenants were women.

****

Chapter 15

Germany

December 9, 1944

"Ginny, by now you know we have moved and I'm glad to report that we are now — somewhere. This 'somewhere' is quite different. Our living quarters aren't too bad except they have year around air conditioning. Utilities are also simplified. The power supply for heat and light is the little, long burning, German candle.

Last night it was so cold, everyone was in bed at 6:30. Tonight we're doing better. Half of us are still up and its seven o'clock."

****

I was up in the Hurtgen Forest today with Graham and Wolf. Never have I been in such a dense forest. It is heavily mined. Our 331st tried to advance today. They captured 22 but paid a grievous price. It's difficult to find room to raise your rifle. I can't imagine waging a battle under these night like conditions.

Some officers thinking is hard to figure out. Major Smith wanted a permanent KP to serve the officers. Lt. Gilman refused to carry out the Major's order and he is now confined to his tent. It looks like our good Lt. is a goner. (The problem was resolved two days later. The Lt. was aware that Army regulations didn't allow KPs to be so used in a war zone. A Private did volunteer after an offer of a weekly salary.)

Our little artillery group has moved up to Bad Stolberg. It was quite a sight as we made our rounds up by the Roer river. This is very flat country and you can see a long way. Two miles back from the river our tanks are dug in every two hundred feet. You can barely see the tops of their turrets. All of the roads behind the tanks are parking lots for endless lines of trucks carrying Navy pontoons. The Germans have flooded the river but it looks like the dash to Berlin is just around that corner.

****

December 12, 1944

"Here's another candlelight date. It's now dark before 5:30; that makes for a long night. These rainy and snowy days are too cold and long. The mud is as bad as ever. Our working conditions are quite difficult. Now I sound like I'm complaining but, believe me, I know we are lucky. At least I can change and get by a warm fire at night. After seeing the 'living quarters' of the troops at the front, one can't feel anything but humble."

****

Gey fell today after bitter house to house fighting. This means the Hurtgen forest is behind us leaving half a dozen small towns along the three mile plain between us and the Roer. Wolf and I both agree, we might get across the Roer and then the Rhine is only thirty miles. For sure the winter will slow our air power and the Germans will fight hard to protect the big cities. We think we're stuck here for the winter.

One thing we do know. Our supplies have caught up to us. The roads leading into Aachen are an amazing sight of an open air warehouse. Crates of ammunition piled five feet high and five feet deep run down both sides of the highway for a couple of miles. I guess this shows the fear we don't have for the German air power.

December 14, 1944

"Well, Ginny, now that you know we are in Germany I guess I can say, 'Yes, we are.' As for the difference between France — total destruction! The few people that are around are quite sad looking. There's no more smiling or waving to do. This morning a little boy said 'Hello' to me but I had to ignore him. Speaking to Germans these days carries a $60.00 fine. For that price I'll stay a little rude."

****

I wrote my brother Al on December 18th. He was always told a little more of the reality. "Of all things the Luftwaffe strafed us today. It's been a long time since we had to duck from a plane. You're all probably worrying about the new attacks of the Germans, but we're worrying about some lost sleep. We don't think any of this will last long."

****

The good news this day was our 329th Infantry actually got across the Roer and into Duren making us the closest troops to Berlin. The 453rd Anti-Aircraft men had all they could handle with the Luftwaffe. They shot down 29 German planes. Who said the Germans were dead?

****

December 21st : "Ginny, we're getting a good tour of 'holy' German homes. Ten of us have moved into a little house outside a quaint village (Mausbach). The building was a war torn mess, but now Wolf has the white, bullet pierced, stove roaring and he's trying to pop some corn. Would you pass the butter please?

If you have been reading about GI feet problems, you don't have to worry about ours. It's the frontline troops that can't get their feet dry. Our feet are being checked almost daily."

****

This German counter attack has taken us by surprise. The rumors are flying that they gained a couple of miles to the south of us and we could be retreating off this point. One lone plane strafed us and Lt. Norton became so excited he called out the whole company. We stayed in a cramped guarding position for the whole, brutal night.

Poor Bond is hoping to get a Christmas pass to visit his girl in Luxembourg. Now, we're hoping they don't have us headed in that direction. One thing for sure, this will be a new Christmas experience.

Saturday, December 23, 1944

"Ginny, you'll be glad to know your bathroom on a Saturday night isn't the most hectic place in the world. We have been packing and unpacking all day but then the same thing happened yesterday. Bond said, 'That's it. I'm putting my cot in a neutral zone — out on the road.'

Here's an interesting experience your Dad will enjoy. Yesterday, while driving down a road, the sound of a fighter caught my attention. Looking up I saw a Thunderbolt right on the tail of a German plane. The planes were so low the short burst of the Thunderbolt's machine gun was plainly heard. It was exciting to be in a ringside seat. However, something was indeed strange. This German plane didn't have a propeller on either of its two engines. It was too big for a Buzz bomb. Wolf spoke the question we were thinking, 'What the hell's that?' Graham remarked, 'Do you hear the whine of that thing?' The plane was smoking but, as we spoke, it stopped smoking and it zoomed off like a rocket. Our Thunderbolt was left sitting there like a dumb dodo. We just sat with our mouths hung open.

On arriving home we excitedly told the Lt. and Bond. They looked at one another and sadly shook their heads. Fine friends, but the Stars and Stripes saved us. It has been our privilege to have seen the Germans new plane, a 'Jet.' The engines suck air in and blow it out at a much faster speed. Man they are fast! At this stage of the war it's doubtful if they have very many. Let's hope not.

Our doughboys captured a Chaplain today who said the Germans are going to hit us hard and drive us back. If they fail, they will surrender on December 24. What a nice Christmas story. Should I hang my socks out now? A Nazi Chaplain wouldn't lie, would he? By the time you get this you will have the answer."

****

Christmas Eve,1944

"Well, Hon, here's another Christmas and quite a different one. To visualize this scene just imagine the first Christmas. It's not exactly a manger, but we are bunked down over the top of a stable. It's not as bad as it may sound. Thanks to our generator our bulbs are a little brighter than our morale. — It's just Christmas.

On the lighter side I volunteered again. The cold has numbed my brain was Doggett's quote. Anyway, we were moving and we had this rare vehicle in for repair. It's called a 'Weazel.' It looks like a small tank without the turret. It also drives like a tank. You steer using right and left hand levers which in turn control either of the tracks. The floor is vacant except for the necessary gas pedal. All one had to do was get the feel of the levers. Ha.!

Behind the Weazel they attached Lt. Gilman's private, quarter ton trailer. Off we went with Dog and Bond driving the trucks behind me. After the first mile I realized Dog's quote was right. Not only was I freezing in this open air vehicle but it was real work to keep the darn thing on the snow and ice covered road. These were hilly, winding roads. At a curve I went up one bank, down across the road and up the other bank. Dog and Bond were blowing their horns in laughter so I didn't look back. I raised my hand in victory. On the next straightaway I glanced over my shoulder and sure enough they were laughing again. The poor Lt's. trailer was following me upside down. I'm trying to remember the words he used on me but, no matter, he would cut them out. Thankfully, because of the snow there wasn't much harm done, Sir.

The roads got better and so did my coordination until an Army truck tried crossing my path at an intersection. I pulled back as hard as I could on both levers hoping the tracks would grab something. By sheer luck I missed him, some Germans and a telephone pole. This stopped the convoy and once again I received a jolly round of laughter. Me and the Weazel were tangled up in a bunch of loose wires. Bond leaned out his window and yelled, 'Hey, Rags, when are you going to volunteer again?'"

****

Christmas day started with snow squalls. Rumors of the German counterattack and our future were a dime a dozen. Earl Graham and I had some left over repair work so after a quick, K ration breakfast we headed for the front. The guns were positioned overlooking the last hill to Duren. For a Christmas treat a group of P47s strafed and bombed the old city, then a Messerschmidt won a dogfight with a P47. We held our breath until a parachute opened. Luckily the pilot just made it over the river. It was a good feeling to see him get up and hop into a Jeep.

Working on the gun sights, in this weather, has become a team effort. Graham removes his helmet and I remove my gloves. No matter how much I blow on my hands I'm sure to lose one screw to Graham's safety netted helmet. The reward for our numb fingers were worth it. The artillery fed us a great, hot turkey lunch.

When we returned to our manger everyone was all packed, just waiting for the order, "Pull out!" Fortunately, the mess truck was going full blast putting out our Christmas dinner. Since this was my second one, I didn't pig out. I took two legs and washed them down with two cups of good egg nog, without the stick.

A group of us were sitting around our little stove when Santa arrived in the form of Lt. Gilman. Somehow he had a bottle of scotch, gin and brandy. After a shot of our choice, we got into a typical Army bull session. For sure we were shocked at the strength of the German attack. And we also knew that it was possible we could be cut off if we didn't retreat. Our upcoming move had to be a retreat to Belgium. Musser remarked, "Boy, the way you guys are talking and the looks of this weather, it seems like a replay of Valley Forge." Nobody laughed.

Two hours later we were in the worst convoy of all time. There was only one highway in use and it was bumper to bumper. A few times we stalled for an hour. This left a group of us to gather in Bond's winterized truck. On one occasion I stepped out on the tailgate to relieve myself. Looking up at the hazy sky I was shocked to see a German plane diving straight down my throat. I yelled and dove off into a snow bank waiting for the rat-a-tat-tat of his machine guns. This brought everyone else out to relieve themselves. He must have been empty but we thought for sure other planes would attack us sitting ducks.

Traveling through Aachen we wondered about the open air, ammunition warehouse along this highway. The first bridge gave us our answer. All the ammunition was thrown in the creeks.

This convoy seemed like a never ending bad dream. The going was painfully slow, it was damn cold, dark and we had no idea where we were going. As dawn broke we pulled into the village of Mauerlange, Belgium. In twelve hours we had journeyed eighty miles. Here they had ten inches of snow on the ground and I thought of our poor infantry. Theirs was a longer trip with no winterized trucks with stoves, and now they'll have to fight and sleep in this winter wonderland. It goes without saying, none of us will forget this Christmas day of 1944.

****

Chapter 16

Battle Of The Bulge

No sooner had I unloaded my barracks bag when, along with Wolf and ten others, we were ordered to pack light for yet another little trip. There were some needed supplies waiting in Liege. Before we could groan, our baggy eyes lit up. The Sgt. was saying, "You'll be staying in a hotel." As it turned out, the two nights turned into a mini vacation. We got warm, had a hot shower and there were real girls serving us meals. It seemed like a piece of heaven until suddenly there came raids of Buzz bombs. A Buzz bomb attack is an unusual experience. The first one caught us by surprise. I was playing table tennis at the Red Cross. At the first sound of the approaching bomb everyone in the crowded club went completely motionless and silent. It resembled a stuck movie film. After the explosion, it was like a switch was thrown; we all resumed playing like nothing had occurred.

That night six, rumbling bombs kept me sleeping with one eyebrow up. Blocks and blocks of Liege have been leveled by the Buzz bomb. For these civilians war is also hell.

Riding back in an open Jeep was a freezing experience. So we stopped in a little village and jumped around a bit. Much to our surprise this brought out the villagers who dragged us into their homes, sat us by a warm stove and gave us a cup of brew, quite a change from Company routine.

When we reached the Company area it was no surprise to find the 783rd had moved again. It didn't take long to find them. Nor did it take long to bundle down for the night lying there thinking what a difference one night can make.

For some reason we were now allowed to tell of our moves but not our present location. I wrote Ginny the next day.

"Retreating on that cold Christmas night was a gloomy period. One day we're looking down on our next objective, Duren, and the next day we've retreated through two other countries! This is a heck of a way to be winning a war.

Now the good news. Christmas packages are somehow still getting through. Yours arrived today in perfect condition and your selection will stock up my run down stock of socks, handkerchiefs and gloves. It goes without saying, your Mom's fudge was quickly devoured."

****

January 1, 1945
"Happy New Year, Hon, and who said the war would end last October 15?

My new year could have started better. Like a tap on my shoulder woke me and a distant voice said, 'Guess what? Your on KP!'

We're short handed and it's my first KP since leaving the States. We were having twenty turkeys so I didn't care. I ate turkey and drank egg nog all day. As it turned out, it was an exciting KP. It was almost noon when I heard that dreaded, familiar sound rumbling from the eastern sky. One look skyward and there it was, another Buzz bomb headed for

Leige except this one had to be different. I was leaning on the mess truck which was sitting in an open field. This crazy bomb caught the smell of turkey. The darn thing was coming straight down so I didn't wait around. I sprinted for the end of the street and turning the corner I dove head first. Two little kids were on the first porch, and they liked my act so much, they ran and dove on top of me. With that the bomb exploded.

The earth shook violently. I wasn't sure if our turkeys had survived. I rolled from under the kids and saw the bomb had hit the farmhouse on the other side of our truck. I patted the scared kids on the head and ran for the smoldering house. Sadly an elderly woman was crushed to death.

On returning to KP Gates, the Mess Sgt., took one look at me. 'What the hell happened to you, Rags?' When the kids dove on me they pushed my face into the curb. Now I'm sporting another black eye with two band aids. Needless to say, I lead the Company in black eyes.

It was nice to see normal people again but they can cause problems. At supper I was serving the bread and jelly. Two little kids with big eyes were watching my every move and slowly inched closer. Quietly I slipped them two slices that were loaded with jam. Like magic I now had two chow lines plus the staring, dark gaze of Sgt.Gates."

****

This is the worst fighting of the war. It sounds like we have slowed the German advance but in these bitter conditions no one is sure we have the upper hand. This is cold, mountainous country plus the weather has cancelled our Air Force advantage. We got caught with our pants down and it's going to take awhile to get them buckled up again.

January 6, 1945

"What, my Dear Censor cut a hole in my letter!! This cold weather must be giving him thin skin or else I gave him one needle too many.

Yes, it is cold! Last night Doggett and I were on guard and the artillery fired until six this morning. This was the most artillery we have seen since Normandy. If nothing else, it sure warmed our hearts.

To answer some of your questions — we are fine but we would like it if someone shut off the North Pole air. This morning, as we were repairing the first gun, they showed us a thermometer. It read 9! There have been some frozen feet but mine have been okay. Every once in awhile I go into that Indian war dance you taught me. Now they're concerned on the contents of my head. (Ginny's Grandfather was half Indian.)

As far as our human feelings about the war? Boy, you're getting deep. Of course, we realize there is a possibility of never getting home again, but I honestly haven't had to dwell on that one. I'm sure it's a lot different in the everyday hell of the infantry soldier. For sure I don't believe my name is on a bullet. Just being in the right or wrong spot has a lot to do with our well being. No matter how the cards are stacked, one of these days, I assure you, the sun will rise and your pretty face will gleam with the sunshine of a new day. Now let me get down off the pulpit."

January 9, 1945 — "What a vacation spot; we're on the top of a big hill and for miles around all you see are snow covered evergreens. Momentarily a beautiful sight, then the sound of the artillery and the cold snap you back to reality. To match the swimming pool and the four tennis courts, we have snow suits and snow balls plus a hole in the roof. Six of us are sleeping in the next room, no heat but we do have two light bulbs, two hours a night.

Bond and I both went up to the front today hoping to solve the problem of frosting lens. We're trying to coat them with a solution but that means removing the lenses. You can imagine, under these conditions, that's tough sledding. The fingers stiffen quickly so we take turns. While the one works the other guy blows on his hands and stamps his feet. At first we laughed at one another but now it's all 'damns.' When I see the cardboard holes these fellows are living in, and the infantry up ahead fighting night and day, I will never complain of freezing fingers. What amazes me is the morale and the sense of humor of these gunners."

My twenty-third birthday fell on January 14 and, unbelievably, the mail brought birthday cards, packages and 21 Philly news papers dating from October. None of them had the answer to my question. Where have the last three years gone? The years seem to be dragging and flying at the same time.

On the 17th our little group moved up to St.Antoine to stay close to the guns. " This is another battered house and town. The shell holes got plugged today, now an old drum is giving off some heat. There are five women from another town living in the next room. Trying to talk to them has been almost useless. Two of the older women are very sick. They moaned all night. We can't feed them much, the kitchen isn't with us. It's a pitiful sight.

At dusk a lone tank came rumbling into the village. It was snowing so hard we didn't know if it was ours. Not until it scraped our building, under our noses, were we positive it was a Sherman tank. The scared women huddled in the corner and Wolf looked at me coming up with the Laurel and Hardy comedy line, 'Well, Ollie, this is another fine mess you got us into.'

The Germans have been jamming BBC which means we are lacking in current news. Just today we learned of Patton's army's dash to this front. You should be seeing some writeups on the 83rd. Last night, before the radio squeaked off, we heard the BBC report on our 329th gaining their objective by resorting to trench knives. This morning we learned the number of our men who survived. It was a sad number and they are all in the hospital. Their frozen uniforms had to be cut off. I won't complain of the cold again.

Did you hear my brothers were drinking toasts to me at the Christmas dinner? They were moving me back one city at a time until they had me in Paris. I'm glad someone is having some fun at my expense."

****

A blizzard hit on January 19. "Trees are down on the roads so there is no way to get to the front. This also meant another day without air power. The Germans have sure been lucky with this weather. Since Christmas, there hasn't been any bombing and only piecemeal strafing. The only thing we know is the Germans have to be running out of gas in their gas tanks as well as in physical strength."

January 21st: "Driving on the torn up, snow packed, roads feels like you're in a reducing machine. My head is sore from hitting the roof of the truck. But it looks like this move was worth it. Eight of us are staying in another village and we're sleeping two fellows to a house. The best part, our "home" has a real Mom, real lights, a working stove and a telephone that doesn't work.

The chow has been Spam, Spam, Spam. Somehow we got a big orange with the Spam last night. I gave the orange to Mom. Her eyes lit up like a Christmas tree. This morning she fed us eggs and bacon fried in real butter. Boy, what a treat! From all accounts our armies almost have the Bulge cut off. Last night the BBC commentator reported, 'With the oil on their rifles frozen, with swollen, chapped faces and frozen hands and feet, riflemen of the 83rd Infantry Div. fought continuously in the Artic like climate of the Ardennes Forest for five days and nights, paving the way for the 3rd Armored to cut the vital St.Vith-Houffalixe highway.' This is the same highway we took in September on leaving Luxembourg for Germany.

The Air Force finally got up to the front today. What a beautiful sight. And, Mom just walked over and stoked the fire. Things are really looking up."

****

January 27, 1944
"How do you like this? Lt. Norton just sent us orders.

'All enlisted men, will at all times, salute officers. Everyone will wear the uniform of the day with no three day beards.' Actually, that's good news because it means the Battle Of The Bulge is over!"

****

The following two weeks the Company got back together in one place and we went to work repairing just about everything that was broken. Throughout this time many wild rumors were flying in the winds. One of them came true. In a long convoy the whole Company moved to Maarland, Holland to rest and resupply the weakened 83rd.

When the casualties were released it was apparent why so many of the Divisions were resting. The losses were worse than Normandy. Killed in action 8,000, wounded 48,000, captured or missing 21,000 and a loss of 733 tanks. German losses were put at 90,000, 600 tanks and a surprising 1,600 airplanes.

For some reason, while we were in "hiding," censorship became very tight. My letters didn't begin until February 7th and my clues were rather obvious.

"Each family in the village gladly invited two soldiers in to live with them. Musser and I had a nice double bed with white sheets.

This is a small village without a war scratch and it's not near Paris. The custom around here is you must take off your shoes as you come in the back door.

Last night 'our family,' which is Mom, Dad and a shy fifteen year old daughter, invited us to dinner. Our orders are not to eat with our families but what can you do when they grab your arm and insist. By sign language they showed us two, huge, steaming covered bowls indicating they had an ample supply. Muss said, 'What the heck, let's do it once and then they'll feel better.'

As we sat down, they removed the covers revealing one stacked with boiled potatoes and the other boiled cabbage! A typical long loaf of bread, plus a foreign spread, was passed around. Smiling, gulping and nodding, we managed to get through another once in a lifetime meal.

Every chance we get we bring them food items. At first they refused so Muss and I would simply 'hide' fruit, candy and nuts where they were quickly found. Boy, how soon we

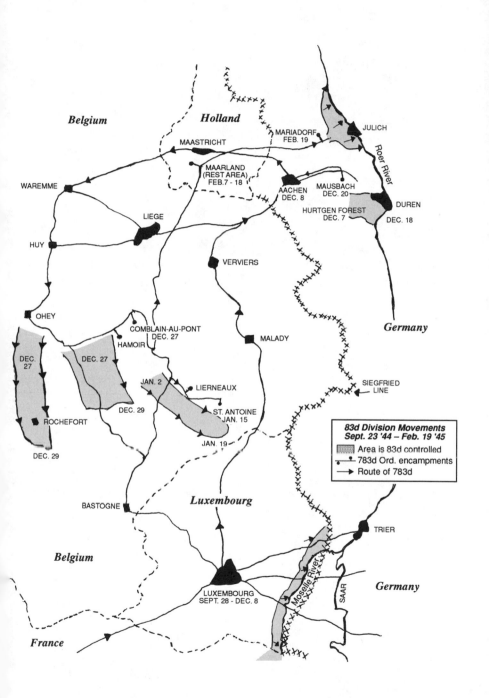

Belgium

Holland

MARIADORF
FEB. 19

JULICH

MAASTRICHT

Roer River

MAARLAND
(REST AREA)
FEB. 7 - 18

WAREMME

AACHEN
DEC. 8

MAUSBACH
DEC. 20

DUREN
DEC. 18

LIEGE

HURTGEN FOREST
DEC. 7

HUY

VERVIERS

OHEY

COMBLAIN-AU-PONT
DEC. 27

MALADY

HAMOIR

DEC.
27

DEC. 27

Germany

JAN. 2

LIERNEAUX

SIEGFRIED
LINE

DEC. 29

ST. ANTOINE
JAN. 15

ROCHEFORT

JAN. 19

DEC. 29

83d Division Movements
Sept. 23 '44 – Feb. 19 '45

▨ Area is 83d controlled

•→ 783d Ord. encampments

→ Route of 783d

BASTOGNE

Luxembourg

TRIER

Belgium

Germany

Moselle River

SAAR

LUXEMBOURG
SEPT. 28 - DEC. 8

France

Battle Of The Bulge — January 1945

take the little pleasures of life for granted. The finding of one candy bar or orange brings forth unbelievable joy."

During this time we continued our routine repair work. It was also class learning time. 'Proper Behavior Towards German Civilians.' Rumors weren't needed to let us know we would soon be leaving to restart the race to Berlin.

On Washington's birthday I told Ginny about our one nagging problem — strained toilet facilities. "The Army solved it in the usual manner. A slit trench in our backyard. This tarp was strung up protecting the house side with a three foot hedge on the other. Squatting early one morning I had to learn that no one had checked to see what was on the other side of that hedge. I almost fell in backwards when a pretty teenage girl came riding by on her bicycle. She waved and with a big smile she said, 'Good Morgen.'" This was the day my constipation started and lasted three weeks."

Living in the homes of the Holland people was a warm and loving experience. Many tears were being shed when we pulled up stakes and headed to Mariadorf, Germany on February 19th.

We are now back with the Ninth Army and, again, our first objective is to get across the Roer River. Just like before, the artillery is dug in all down the line. This time, however, the 29th and 30th Divisions are in front of us. It appears they are going to try to break through and then the 83rd will come up to pass through and make a dash for the Rhine. There is very little snow which should allow the movement of tanks and troops. We shall soon see.

Another sizable shelling began the drive on February 24th. The 29th and 30th Divisions quickly crossed the Roer. The 83rd and the 2nd Armoured Divisions were fully committed. This three prong attack quickly spread out as the Germans slowly gave ground. The Division's mission was to capture the city of Neuss, but a real plum would be capturing a bridge across the Rhine to Dusseldorf.

We moved into Julick on March 1st and I wrote Ginny, "The towns we're going through are totally destroyed. It was a surprise to see some civilians but they turned out to be left behind Russians. Every other girl is pregnant.

After a few spring days, today it is snowing. This has not stopped the Air Force. The Germans are getting pounded and they are retreating. Our morale is high."

The next day I announced to Ginny, "The 83rd has reached the Rhine and we were first! By now you must have read it in the newspapers. Now you and the General won't have to guess where we are."

It was no easy task getting to the Rhine. The four Divisions fought night and day. The Germans fought hard and almost broke through on the right flank of the 331st Regiment. The IX Tactical Air Force gave them a great assist by knocking out twenty tanks. Four hours later the 331st became the first Allied troops to reach the Rhine. Unfortunately, they had no luck in securing one of the three bridges. Just as they approached, the Germans blew the center span.

Their Air Force is continuing to surprise us. Last night they attacked twelve times, with single planes, trying to bomb our pontoon bridge on the Roer River. This morning a jet came whizzing by. Our anti-aircraft guns never came close. Thank heavens they don't have many of these.

March the 3rd and 4th found the Company moving twice ending up in the town of Glenn, three miles from the Rhine. The way we find quarters in Germany is completely different than anywhere else.

"This was one hectic day, Ginny. I left with the advance party early this morning. Four of us were with the Captain and all we had to do was find quarters for 140 men and parking for 40 trucks. After checking out a couple of towns the Captain declared, 'This is it!' And so it goes every day.

The poor civilians don't know what to do. Some run and others hide. For sure no one wants us to chose their home. Reese Phillips, from Olney High, speaks a fair German. He told the first family they had until two to move. A young girl asked, 'Which way do you want us to go?' Reese replied, 'Any way but east.' By the time we climbed back into the Jeep the whole family was out of the house, packs on their backs and marching down the street.

Some days we have a whole square full of people. Most of them simply stare in disbelief but some actually smile. One fellow came running up and wanted to help us unpack declaring, 'Me Pollock.' He probably was but we can't afford to take any chances.

Wolf and I have been playing a game with a German and the chickens in his barn. He goes in checking for eggs some time after us. I don't know who is winning but we now have five fresh eggs. Tomorrow our rules get a little tough. Only one person per household is allowed out to get their food and water but only from nine till noon.

This is great news! We just heard that the first Army has captured the Remagen bridge and we have troops across the Rhine. They are quoting Eisenhower as saying, 'The final defeat of the enemy is just around the corner.'

Our front is so quiet some of the infantry went back to Belgium training for the assault on the Rhine. They're using the Maas river as a practice for the Rhine. It looks like we are going to stay put for awhile.

Later in the week I told Ginny about our journey back to Belgium to pick up new Jeeps. "When we arrived at our present town it was dark and I was asleep. Now as the six of

us climbed into the back of our taxi ambulance, for our trip
to Belgium, I mentioned this fact to Wolf. 'I want to look out
the back window to see how we got in here.' With that
remark I was pushed to the front and sat on until we were
down the the main highway.

After picking up the Jeeps we split up. Wolf and I headed
for our Holland families in Maarland. He went to his house
and I had a pleasing, surprise visit with 'Mom'. Wolf and I
had agreed to meet but somehow we fouled up. He came for
me and I went for him, but we never did find one another. It
was getting later than I liked. Taking off as fast as a new Jeep
would go I had hopes of catching Wolf on the main road to
Aachen. Much to my disbelief the road was completely
empty.

The sun was setting as I tore down the road from Aachen
to Neuss and it was much colder. All I knew was I had to make
a left turn somewhere in the next thirty miles or I'd be in the
Rhine. After some twenty minutes I tried two left turns into
towns but they were blanks. The streets were vacant. While
turning the Jeep around I spotted some Germans peeking
from behind their closed curtains. Flashing through my
mind came a message, 'What a dope, keep driving like this
and you'll get yourself shot.'

A mile down the road I caught a truck but the new driver
only knew his location. Now I was getting anxious. Was I the
last guy on the road? Suddenly a sign appeared, '10 Kms to
Nuess.' For sure I couldn't go much further. Darkness was
definitely setting in as I turned left. Figuring I had about
three miles to go, I tread on the gas. Out of the dusk an S
curve appeared flanked on both sides by large trees. I hit the
brakes and the Jeep spun out on a sheet of ice. We did a
complete circle spinning off the road backwards right be-

tween two huge trees. As I sat there catching my breath I heard that little voice again, 'That was pretty neat; how did you do that?'

Driving off at a much slower pace, two miles down the road, I found the 783rd. I turned off the ignition and was letting out a sigh of relief when all six foot five inches of Sgt. Jones bellowed, 'Where the hell have you been?' I started to explain but he seemed more interested in walking around and feeling my Jeep. He came back, leaned down to my eyeballs and calmly asked,

'Okay, Rangnow, tell me, how in the hell did you miss that row of trees?'

'Trees? What trees?' I asked.' With a slight grin Jones added, 'Well, you're the only guy that made that curve without a dent. Go get yourself a drink before your chattering teeth fall out.'

In the Artillery repair truck I found my drink and a party that had been going on for sometime. Pfeifer's wrecker crew had hauled a barrel of German wine out of a cellar. One swig and I realized why no one was feeling any pain. The telling of my day was greeted with tears of laughter. Sometime later I had the task of getting woozy Bond back to our room through the half frozen mud. Sure enough, we stumbled and down we went in a laughing heap. After getting Gene in bed I noticed I had ripped the knee out of my pants and it was bleeding. To get first aid I went to the orderly room. I was telling Phil Barbara my tale of woe and lowering my pants when Captain Getty entered and yelled, 'What is this, another drunk?' Sgt. Jones spoke right up, 'No, Rangnow doesn't drink. He fell!"

****

After I thanked Jones he told me the Captain was having a bad night. Some of the guys on a guard post had the same wine and they were taking pot shots at the civilians trying to use their outhouses. Six fellows lost their stripes over the wine incident. It was the last time we had flowing spirits until the end of the war.

On March 12th I received a disturbing letter from Ginny. My good friend, Ed Perry, had been shot down. I answered,

"I've always had a scary feeling about Ed. He and Brog both expressed a vague sense of doom. After one bombing run I don't know what other feeling one could have. I'll be hoping and anxiously awaiting some good news on Ed. It would be good to hear that someone saw the crew jump.

The good news is my rich brother and Mildred are getting married. He begged my approval at Christmas. My advice was if he had enough money to give it a try, don't wait for me. He then gave me his opinions in regards to us but I can't go into that now, it's my bedtime."

For the next ten days we did routine work. Some fellows got three day Paris passes while the rest of us watched the daily bombing raids on Dusseldorf. The night attacks were most interesting. The city was close enough for us to plainly see a number of German searchlights sweeping the sky until they targeted a bomber. It resembled a spider catching a silver fly in its web. Of course, the anti-aircraft quickly zeroed in while we rooted for the bomber to swerve out of range. Sometimes we won, but either way, I always thought of Ed. A letter from Mom on the 23rd had some hopeful news on him. "His plane dropped out of formation. They tell me this means he had a chance to jump." I'm hoping.

****

The assault on the Rhine began here on March 24 with a big bombing run which almost blotted out the sun on a cloudless day. It took us another day to learn that Patton, located down river, was already across.

To Ginny, "I have the detailed account from the Stars and Stripes in front of me quoting Eisenhower who watched from a church tower. — 'The assault on the night of March 22-23 was preceded by a violent, artillery bombardment. On the front of the two American Divisions, two thousand guns of all types participated. Because the batteries were distributed on flat plains every flash could be seen. The din was incessant.

At dawn I went to a convenient hill from which I saw the arrival of the airborne units. In the assault there were a total of 1,572 planes and 1,326 gliders. A total of 889 fighters escorted them and 2,153 other fighters provided cover over the target area establishing a defensive screen to the east.

An effective smoke screen was laid down as the planes and paratroopers filled the skies for the most successful airborne operation of the war. The way has been blasted open for the 30th and 79th Divisions by our artillery, and airborne power, to the extent that only thirty-one casualties were sustained during the crossing of the Rhine.'

All this good news has our morale at an all time high. This time I really think the Germans are going to run out of breath as we chase them to Berlin. But, don't bet yet!

Your palm reading was interesting but my being home by June is a little too much. As for getting married shortly after — I can't go into that now — it's my bedtime."

****

Chapter 17

The Race To Berlin

The Company was packed early the next morning. By noon we had moved to the river bank at Meers. And, there we sat all afternoon. With a typewriter, that I had picked up in a bombed out factory, I dashed off a V letter to Ginny.

"Again we are sitting and waiting to move. We don't know where or how far we are going. The tough part is driving on these roads without lights."

I was assuming that Ginny might read through the lines. It was 1:22 a.m. when we crossed the Rhine and the anticipation was greater than the event. The very long convoy was moving at a snail's pace. It was an extremely dusty road but the full moon made the road visible.

It was almost four o'clock when we pulled to the side of the road. Sleeping was out of the question so I went back to Bond's truck, got out some candles and we read some old Philadelphia Evening Bulletins until dawn.

A funny thing was we were allowed to write but the date and location had to be omitted. It was March 31st.

"We are moving constantly without much sleep. Last night we just slept on the ground and tonight who knows. All is utter confusion. There is artillery on our left and right. Trucks and equipment are flying in every which direction.

The rumors are thicker than ever and all the radio tells us is 'there's a blackout on information.' We do know that Frankfort fell to the 3rd Army two days ago. This means we have a solid 150 mile front across the Rhine. The cry now is

'Three hundred miles to Berlin!'"

****

We are on the outskirts of Lundinghausen.

April 2, 1945

"Here is your wandering, groggy boy who is hoping to get his first good night's sleep in ten days. We have set a record, we haven't moved in ten hours! Yesterday was Easter. The moves started at four in the morning and by mid-afternoon we had chalked up three new locations. Of all things they told us we could go to church. It sure seemed odd to be sitting in a church with a whole bunch of soldiers singing with a real organ.

An hour after returning we were in convoy seeing unbelievable sights. People are simply streaming back on both sides of the highway, former captured French soldiers waving and yelling, followed by pathetic looking civilians. Most of them are men and they are all plodding to somewhere. What they are eating is a mystery to us. We did pass some butchered horses.

All the homes are flying white flags. The Germans are standing in their doorways watching this mass movement with disbelief written all over their somber faces.

The dial telephone is still working in this house. Wolf has been dialing any old number and when someone answers he shouts some unprintable German cuss words.

Our meals, surprisingly, have held up well. Tonight it was chicken and chocolate cake but tomorrow it's back to C and K rations.

Our first rainy day in weeks hit us on April 4th. "The gale winds stopped us but it's giving us the chance to at least wash some underwear.

You see all kinds of odd sights. Dog and I saw a German Major, followed by two Privates, walking down the center of the street, through the heart of town, passing an M.P. who didn't give the parade a second look. In the next town a German officer was in the middle of the main intersection directing traffic. It's getting to be a strange war.

A little further on we spotted a deer, at the edge of the woods, a hundred yards away. One of the guys in the back of the truck begged for my rifle. I didn't stop and would you believe he got the deer with three shots. The poor walking civilians didn't know what to think. Most of them dove into the ditch.

Somehow the Mess Sgt. picked up another 600 pounds of German hot dogs. I'm hoping he knows how to cook deer or my next letter might begin with a bark.

Your Dad will be interested in our find of a huge German gun. Measuring it with my feet it was 64 feet from breech to muzzle. Its shell was 380mm and it stood four feet tall. It appeared they were surprised because they only had time to blow up one of its turning motors. Alongside the railroad track was the biggest soldier I have ever seen. He was German and he was dead. He was well over six feet without his cleanly, cut off head. That's measuring him with my feet.

The whole Division has been moving at such a pace, we haven't been able to set up to do battle. I haven't touched a screwdriver in over a week. Things will change when we hit a mountain range or a river."

The best news was coming from the Stars and Stripes. We were well aware that the whole war wouldn't end with the fall of Berlin.

The invasion of Okinawa sounds like another D day using 1200 ships to land 180,000 troops. If nothing else this war is upgrading our geography. I wasn't sure where that island was floating. Its size of 60 by 350 miles is small but it's going to take a lot of lives to get out the dug in Japs.

Two days later we moved the whole Company into two, very large, luxurious homes. "Each has six bedrooms and all are equipped with a sink. The big surprise, we got running water. We have plugged our generator into the electric water heater. The biggest, deepest bathtub I have ever seen is just waiting for its first American soldier. Of course, this will go by rank. I'm hoping someone will splash a little hot water on me.

Today, standing guard, a young girl ran to me shouting, 'The Russians are shooting.' I stopped two M.Ps who took her to the field. Sure enough two Russians, with guns, had a scared German digging his own grave. Then this morning, right before dawn, our trip flare went off. I ran down the road to check and spotted a figure coming up the road. When he saw me he took off across the field. Little did he realize he was up against a star, broken field runner. I dashed back around the block and got on the opposite side of the field. As he tripped over the fence I towered over him. He a-rose with his hat in his hand stuttering, 'Comrade, comrade!'

While marching him back to the guardhouse he kept on repeating he lived in the house over yonder. When he observed me picking up the phone, to summon Sgt. Jones, he burst out sobbing and groaning. The bleary eyed Sgt. picked up his phone to hear me shouting, 'Oh shut up!' This brought a proper question in reply, 'Well, what the hell's the matter with you?' He laughed when I filled him in and he came right down. When the guy saw the size of Jones and the set of his face he wailed all over again. This was too much for Jones who ranted right back at the sad sack and he sent him scampering for home.

The Division was given the green light on April 4th to take off with the 2nd Armored Division to form our own spearhead for the race to Berlin. Our location is outside Ahlen, some sixty miles east of Dusseldorf.

A short letter was dashed off on April 7th. "We are moving shortly and I failed to tell you about our bathrooms! They not only have two toilets but one is male, making the the other female. The females have hot and cold handles for spraying water. The rest I will leave to your imagination! Moe Debic was targeted and told, 'Moe, you just have to try the feel of this neat seat.' Poor Moe just about relaxed. Wolf gave him both handles. Moe reacted like a shot from a mortar. We are going to miss this fun house."

****

It has now become impossible to maintain the artillery. Our spearhead has advanced thirty miles in three days. We are using every truck we can lay our hands on to try to keep up with the tanks. Right now the infantry is sixty miles ahead of us and our chant is, "Go, go, go!"

April 8, 1945
"Another long, interesting move but it's late and I'm writing by candlelight. This evening a Jeep load of us toured a hidden airport with an experimental tank shop. The planes were cleverly hidden under the trees with a grass field serving as the runway. The landscape is southern New Jersey

including sandy soil. I counted thirty damaged planes hidden behind a mock up of houses, windmills and cows.

The tank factory was the biggest surprise. Here, in an innocent little building, stood the biggest tank imaginable.

It didn't have its turret but it still towered over us, and its tracks were twice as wide as a normal tank. We were still chattering about this as we entered the next building. All of our mouths dropped open. Sitting there was a self-propelled gun which made the tank look small. We measured it at eleven feet high and thirty eight feet long. One can't deny the fact that the Germans have the best equipment and now it seems they were on to the largest. Our tank guns are just now getting to be a match with the 88. The majority of our success is because we have the Germans outnumbered with artillery, tanks and our huge superiority in the air.

Arriving back at our new home we were startled to see another unusual sight and sound. Across the street from us, in a field, is a camp of freed Russians. Our 'boys' were marching over there, eyes front, doing close order drill, while blowing and banging away at a bunch of 'found' instruments. It took awhile before the Russians caught on and laughed. Some just tilted their heads and I could imagine them thinking, 'These Americans are crazy.'"

****

This is turning into a crazy war. Our spearhead advanced another twenty miles today as we crossed the Seine river. The 2nd Armored's nickname is "Hell On Wheels." Now we are sharing the headlines as "The Rag Tag Circus." This is because the Division is using every kind of a vehicle, including anything that is German, to keep up with the 2nd's tanks that are rolling on our right flank.

April 10, 1945

"It sure feels good to sit back and relax with you. These roads are the worst yet. They remind me of the dust bowls out west in the 30s. As we roar through these little towns the poor civilians scatter like sheep. They thought their war was over, but now they're eating dust. But we pay the price too. I just looked in the mirror and I honestly didn't know myself. My entire face and hair were ashen gray. Every night I stick my head in a helmet of water so I can tell who I am. You girls are so lucky to have hair washing nights.

Now you can dust me off again. Wolf and I were sitting up here on the second floor writing, when out of the blue comes this 'Rat-a-tat-tat' of a machine gun followed by the roar of a low flying plane. We dove under the beds. Then we grabbed our rifles and tore down the stairs to the street just in time to see an FW 109 diving at us. It was another dive into a ditch before we jumped up and fired after the plane. He made seven passes at us. Our only damage was a few riddled trucks. He was lucky because I was just getting the hang of leading him when my carbine jammed. Down the road Major Smith, with a few drinks under his belt, came out and stood in the middle of the street firing his pistol. I think the pilot figured any enemy that dumb is better alive."

The terrain has changed to hilly with many more wooded areas. Our 330 Inf. Regiment pulled up to the base of the Hartz mountains today and met stiff resistance. This will slow things up for us but I'm amazed that, in the ten days since crossing the Rhine, we have penetrated one hundred and fifty miles. For the first time it's not just a joke. We might still beat the Russians to Berlin!

Sunday, April 15

"Well, Hon, do you still remember me? Since Wednesday we have been on the run and moving so fast, and often, that half the time I don't know where we are.

Wednesday we emptied all the equipment from our trucks onto the ground. The Captain then asked for volunteers to drive them. Charlie Rohrer twisted my arm, 'These trucks are going up to the front of the Spearhead; you'll be sitting back here cleaning binoculars.' For once Charlie made sense. I walked in to our Dear Lt. and he promptly said, 'No Way!' I pleaded my case and mentioned the fact that he wouldn't have to censor any of my letters. Half an hour later we were driving a six by six and I was trying to get the hang of double clutching the darn thing.

After a few hurry ups and waits, Charlie and I began to get second thoughts. It was now night, in fact it was ten thirty, and we had been waiting for three hours. Suddenly a Lt. climbed aboard declaring, 'Let's go!' He was taking us to his troops in the next town. Pulling up to a long row of houses he matter-of-factly pointed at two houses and said, 'My men are there; go in and kick feet and shout, 'Let's go.' I sure didn't feel comfortable with this command. My group were curled up all over the floor. The rude awakening made them sound more miserable than their crummy appearance. The poor guys slowly climbed into the truck after which we slowly drove out of town.

The moon was just going down. I asked the Lt. where we were going and he answered, 'You'll see in a minute.' Sure enough I picked up the outline of three tanks. The Lt. called for a halt, hopped out, and went to the tanks parked in a field. Within the minute the Lt. was walking back to us and the tanks were pulling on the road in front of me. We had a nice little parade of three tanks and three trucks full of sleepy, grumpy infantrymen. I turned to Charlie and said, 'This is a fine mess you got us into, Ollie.' Charlie's reply was a weak chuckle.

That was the start of a long, dirty and noisy night. It was now pitch dark so I had to stay right behind the last tank or he would simply disappear. As we got close to a town we would stop and the men would disembark. The tanks fanned out closely followed by the infantry. Charlie and I stood, rifles in hand, hoping no German tanks were being awakened by the noise and smelled sweet revenge. In some of the towns there was quite a bit of small arms fire but the infantry never came back with any prisoners. For sure we did not see any civilians either.

Going through the villages was the toughest part. The dust was so bad it was impossible to see the tanks rear cat eyes. A few times I wandered off the road and up a curb. The boys in the rear, in clear Army slang, would inform me exactly what they thought of my driving. Finally, we put in the old Luxembourg plan. Charlie and the Lt. would look up at the tops of the buildings and then tell me, 'A little left, hold it, etc.' It worked and the rightful mutterings from the rear ceased.

It was sometime after midnight. We were awaiting for the return of a patrol of six men. Charlie and I had walked up to the leading tank. It was playing a radio and much to our surprise a newsman broke in to announce, 'President Roosevelt is dead!' Boy, I thought, I am going to be the bearer of important news so I hurried back to the trucks to tell the troops. Instead of the expected surprised reaction, just one soldier spoke up, 'Who the hell cares; let's get out of this damn place!' This drove home another truth of war.

Infantry soldiers exist in a very narrow world whose greatest concern is taking care of themselves so that they might live to see another dawn.

The sun finally came up and we stopped outside another unknown town. Charlie and I went over and sat up against a tree eating a K ration. He said my eyes looked like red road maps and I returned the compliment, 'You look like a gray ghost.' Driving twenty feet behind three tanks, with our windshield down, gave us the look of dusted zombies. Just as I laid my aching head back against the tree the Lt. spoke familiar words, 'Let's go!'

It was only a drive of five miles before a new sight met our tired eyes. Here was a huge field of German prisoners. Our job was to take them thirty miles to the rear. They were crammed into the truck standing so tightly they could not fall down or raise an arm to scratch their noses. Poor Charlie got the worst of the deal. He had to stand on the seat facing the prisoners with his carbine. Now he was leery whether I could drive in a straight line.

It was late afternoon when we made out final trip. I had never felt so bushed but there was this happy glow. It is now apparent, as a fighting force, the Germans are through. We were humbled seeing what it was like, for one day, to live the weary, nerve wracking day of an infantry soldier. There isn't enough money or glory to repay these men for the hardships they've had to endure. For about the hundredth time the thought crossed my mind, we really were lucky to have landed in the 783rd Ord. Co."

****

The word just came back. The 83rd has not only reached the Elbe river but we have two bridges across it. Already the 329th and the 331st Regiments, plus the entire 329th Field Artillery are now in positions less than fifty miles from Berlin. Our "Rag Tag Circus" has completely outrun everyone except the 2nd Armd. The Germans, with the shadows of Berlin on their backs, fought fiercely driving the 2nd Armd. back across the river. Our two divisions were then combined and we held off a furious counterattack on our bridgehead. Now everything is quiet; this may have been the Germans last gasp. From here to Berlin it's mostly plains.

As I think about this drive, it amazes me. In Normandy we were counting our gains in hundreds of yards per day. In the last thirteen days the 83rd has crossed five rivers and gained 280 miles! For an Infantry Division this must be some kind of a record.

Our quarters are now in the undamaged town of Halberstad, which is just four miles from the Elbe.

April 16, 1945

"Boy I feel great! I just had me a bath, which was about two weeks late. This home is undamaged, rather nice, a wee bit fancy, but no running water.

We heard the 83rd's exploits on the British radio so I assume you and the General know our whereabouts. I'll bet you're both excited now. Late this afternoon I stood on the Truman Bridge looking across the Elbe and I found it hard to realize that Berlin was so close. Some 83rd patrols have gone in another ten miles without meeting any resistance. German soldiers and civilians are streaming back to reach our lines. In spite of easy pickings it looks like we might just hold here until the other Divisions and our much needed supplies of food, ammo and gasoline catch up.

The real reason for going to the river was an odd one. As every town is captured the population is given just two hours to turn in all weapons. Your Dad would love to see these beautiful, hand engraved swords and rifles. We are not allowed to mail them home so they get the 'wrap it around the tree' test. They all fail, so into the river they go as our huntsmen sadly shake their heads."

****

For some reason Rohrer and I are on a ten minute alert. Our mortars are in bad shape but we can't understand our standby alert. Maybe there are plans to make a run at Berlin. The radio is broadcasting the President's funeral. It is a shame he didn't live to see the final victory. Oddly his dying has created little discussion. We're assuming all bases were covered at the Yalta conference. Truman must be shocked at this drastic turn in his life.

As we waited I wrote Ginny describing the afternoon events on guard duty. "Three excited 'Poles' came up to me and reported that there were two German soldiers in the house across the street. Very quietly we entered the house and, sure enough, we caught two sixteen year old kids with their pants down. They were in the midst of changing into civilian clothes. To the brig they went.

A half hour later a young girl, with tears streaming down her face, got across to me that her father had just died and they wanted to use the church. Lastly, here came an angry German woman. Her excited jabber was about a fast Russian who stole her pig. In this town guard duty expires very fast. A new guard post is the town store. Their food supply is limited. A natural fear is easily read on their drawn faces. So a guard is posted to remove any thoughts of town rioting.

The Pacific war is drawing a lot of our attention. We are a little dismayed at the slow progress on Okinawa and the heavy toll the Jap suicide planes are causing. Those people are nuts which makes for tough battles. It looks like that war is going to go on for a long time."

****

Another little letter was written on April 20 thanking Ginny for another package. "Boy, hardly a cracker was broken and your gift of a Yo-Yo, for the Lt., was a great idea. He will adore it and we all agreed it was very thoughful of you to think of his childish traits.

Old Doggett just brought in another tankful of Elbe River water. It tastes like iodine. No one drinks it but it's in the food. As for the fighting, we don't know anything. By now we thought we would be pushing on to Berlin, but we're just sitting here twiddling our thumbs. All the other fronts are still moving and at this rate they'll soon run out of land to capture. Except for many by-passed pockets of resistance, the Germans have lost the will to carry on. Driving back to a depot today sure seemed odd. For mile after mile we never saw a single GI. It gave me the feeling that the 83rd was sitting out on the end of a large limb. Fortunately, the Germans are having problems cracking twigs.

You have probably been aware that the censoring of our letters of late has been quite liberal. Now, however, in order to prevent another 'holey' letter, I can only say this: tomorrow Wolf and I are going to escort the Lt. to a train station. For some reason this is a military secret and I might be gone a day or two. This should turn out okay; this time, I didn't volunteer."

****

Lt. Gilman's military secret was he had to report to a school in Britain. When Wolf and I returned on April 24th I wrote Ginny the details of our Laurel and Hardy trip.

"Our mission was to drive the Lt. to Munster where he was to catch a train for Paris. He just missed the train. We quickly tried the airport, no planes. The Lt.'s deadline left us with no choice. We had to drive him back to a nice familiar city, Liege. At this airport it was the same answer — no planes. We were gearing ourselves for the long ride to the fun city — Paris — when the Lt. met a Colonel with a seat in his car. It was after midnight as we bid the Lt. farewell. Our long thirteen hour drive, of 427 miles, was over and we headed for the nearest hotel.

Sunday we were just going to bum around town, but for some reason the MPs didn't like the looks of Wolf. As we were eating a nice breakfast they interrupted giving us a dumb lecture. They didn't like Wolf carrying a knife in his rifle belt. After lunch we went to our room for a bit of a nap. All hell broke loose. The pounding on the door almost knocked us out of bed. Three big MPs busted in, and in a flash, we jumped to our feet. Can you imagine, they wanted to know if we belonged to the Jeep parked out in front of the hotel. Wolf proudly stuck out his Ohio chest and said, 'We sure do!'

'Well, you can't park a Jeep with a loaded machine gun and you'll have to turn over that loaded Tommy gun and the Carbine!' Our guns were beside the bed leaning against the wall. We grabbed them before they took a step. Wolf was now wide awake and he shouted back,

'Just hold it; we're really not the enemy!' However, we got the message. This war had long passed old Liege. We were ducks out of water. They escorted us to our Jeep and then we left them at the curb shaking their heads like WE were nuts.

We headed straight to Holland to our January families. The word of our arrival spread quickly. Suddenly we were the center of attention in a packed house of happy people. They asked where we were fighting and, when we told them we were across the Elbe, there was a chorus of "Ahs" and then cheers with slaps on the back. Talk about your heroes— we were it for the night. Their life of hardship and freedom created our wonderful experience. I'll never forget it.

We had no food so we had to accept their kind dinner offer. Once again it was potatoes. The four adults each ate six large spuds. They kept insisting we take another potato, but how many gravyless spuds can one eat?

Two hours later Wolf dragged me over to greet 'his' family and within the hour we were again eating potatoes! Hon, would you look up that old saying; I have a bet with Wolf that it's from Holland. I believe it goes, 'You look like you have potatoes growing out of your ears.'

Wolf never told me 'his' family was blessed with two teenage daughters. They spoke good English and naturally they were very interested in Americans. They had us writing out the lyrics of all the latest tunes. The hardest part was acting like we knew them. After a little wine and snacks it was suddenly midnight. All kinds of invitations were trying to get through our potato clogged ears. The girls had big double beds, but I insisted that Wolf sleep with me in my 'home.' The Dutch are smart; they keep one, alert eye on their girls. Who can blame them; these guys from Ohio are all Wolfs!

It was heaven nestling between clean, white sheets and our heads sunk in soft, pink pillows. We died until nine and then died again when we saw the dirty mess our crummy hair had left on the pillows. Outside it looked like it was going to pour rain so we allowed our hosts to twist our arms. We stayed for two more good meals, no spuds! The girls kept insisting it was no day to start such a long trip, but with our helmets over our hearts, we announced that duty came first. It was on to Berlin!

Again the whole street came out to say, 'Goodbye, come back again.' Neighbors gave us notes to pass on to the boys who stayed with them. It was truly a great, warm feeling which was quickly washed away when the heavens opened up in Aachen. Still a long way from home we pushed on to Munster, then bedded down for the night. Our unusual, interesting trip, of 889 miles, ended this afternoon with the delivering of the Dutch notes to a bunch of surprised guys.

Now I can tell you that our elation of the war soon ending was dealt a cruel blow on the day before we left. Three of our fellows were on a 'fun trip.' A routine run to the same Supply Depot I visited last week. As they were winding their way through hilly, tree country they were ambushed. Sadly, Bob Moore and Andy Chavis were killed and Ralph Helenthal is seriously wounded. It took Lt. Brown three days to find everyone and get all the facts. These were three great guys and you can imagine such a tragedy puts a somber face on the entire Company. This incident was the reason our Jeep had a mounted machine gun.

Our journey started the day after the ambush and we had to travel the same road. As the forest area came into view, we stopped and prepared ourselves. I released the swivel lock on the machine gun mount and unlocked the safety. The Lt. likewise released his Tommy gun and said, 'Let's go.' Wolf floored the Jeep and we spent the next ten minutes zooming over hill and dale, holding on while keeping an eye for any movement. It was a piece of cake with just a little spicy flavor.

The return trip was of little concern. We figured the pockets of resistance would be cleaned up. Neither did we take any chances. I unlocked our Belgium trouble maker and aimed it straight over Wolf's head."

On returning the news was great. The British have taken over Bremen while Patton's tanks are entering Austria. The Russians are surrounding Berlin, but it looks like the Germans are fighting to the last man. For us it's now evident we're sitting it out waiting for the white flag to go up. Our last 83rd battle was fought behind us in the Hartz mountains. The 330th Regiment stayed and cleaned up that pocket of resistance and took an unbelievable 60,000 prisoners.

On the 26th Charlie Rohrer and I went up to fix those mortars. The 'Doughboys' said their daily patrols are going to within forty miles of Berlin. They see nothing but people streaming back. We stood on the river bank watching all types of humans trying to float or swim the river. Others were trying to crawl across the downed bridge. It's a sorry sight to watch this war on humanity.

All the letters I was receiving were ones of joy about the impending war's end. So here I was again preaching from my pulpit. "For sure we will be doing some shouting, but it won't last long. Our training for Japan is already in the books and we may not be coming back to the states. Your brother, being in a small outfit, is a different case. The war's end is going to cause a lot of frustration and I'd rather see you getting a surprise than a disappointment. You can be sure all those funny rumors will again be coming out of the woodwork.

Up with the artillery today we learned they haven't fired a round in over a week. But, they told us, from the Rhine to the Elbe, they fired 10,000 rounds. Believe me, that is a lot of ammunition moving so fast and far. They are hoping we become an Army of Occupation. Why? They figure they've fired enough. It would be better to put in six months over here and then come home for good. We shall see."

April 30th: Bond found a case of champagne under a hay stack. It's now under his bed waiting for the V Day celebration. Reports are being heard that Hitler is dead and the Russians have one and a quarter million men, supported by twenty two thousand artillery pieces, surrounding weary Berlin. The flag has to go up soon.

To Ginny: "Yesterday we met the Russians. It was no big deal but it was weird. These guys looked more like Civil War veterans. They sure were a motley crew wearing all kinds of mixed uniforms with various styled hats and not a single helmet. They arrived in old, horse drawn, wooden buggys. What a sad version of the 'Big Red Machine.' But, the oddest part was their lack of emotion. We're all smiling and trying to shake hands while most of them just stood with blank faces. That doesn't make any sense, and after seeing that behavior, I don't trust them. They are from another world. Maybe General Patton wasn't too far off with his latest remark. You read it, I guess. 'Let's keep right on going and wipe out these Russian S.O.B.s. We'll have to do it sooner or later and it might as well be now!'

After getting a look at the Russians, and seeing their reactions, I think the General just might be right."

****

May 2, 1945

"The radio is telling us Berlin has fallen but Bond's bottles are still under his bed. I think the bottles will be empty by the time you read this!

Are you staying up on Ike's fraternization rules? It's a $65.00 fine if your get caught talking to a German. And, if you're caught visiting, it can be up to ten years in jail plus a dishonorable discharge! My guess is you're not seeing too much of this in the newspapers. Unfortunately, there have been a few soldiers already who have been snagged by the short skirt.

Now the Infantry, they are a different case. There were times when they were living with civilians and they would help one another. However, if things in a town didn't go well, like snipers, you would never know these were the same men. The civilians were gone. War is hell.

With us service troops things are a lot different. The civilians know who we are and they are no longer scared of the Americans. But, we play it straight by not having a thing to do with anyone. Those that look French or Russian get the same treatment. The only time we talk to any of the civilians is while we are on guard duty. This may be a surprise to you, but this is the way it has been since our first day in Germany.

Doggett gets funnier by the week. Driving through town today he spotted a couple walking hand in hand. Giving me an elbow he asked, 'Rags, you know what that is?'

Innocently I said, ' No, what?'

'That's love, you remember don't you?'

'Of course, I do Art. And, very shortly you and Millie will be doing that and much more.'

His quick, loud reply had something to do with bulls!"

****

Monday, May 7, 1945

"There hasn't been any official announcement, but we think this is the Victory in Europe Day that we've been looking for. All the corks on the champagne have been popped but everyone is staying quite calm. It's another case where the anticipation is greater than the real thing. Now if the announcement was, 'Your leaving for home in a month,' we'd have a real party.

The Stars and Stripes are reporting that half the combat troops will receive furloughs in the States before going to the Pacific. Please don't put any credibility in upcoming newspaper reports. They could be half truths, but you know Army orders constantly change. It will be big rumor time all over again.

One sure bet will be that our free style of Army life will soon end. The days of the garrison soldier, drilling, roll calls and spit and polish will soon descend on us. It will be accompanied with moans and groans.

In the nearby canal Doggett found a boat. So we capped this great day by celebrating like two little kids, paddling ourselves in circles."

****

The Stars And Stripes answered many of our lingering questions with front page headlines of the 83rd.

"The Rag-Tag Circus — They Make History"

The article stated, "using any kind of transportation you can name; German cars, fire engines, farmers' wagons, bicycles and an airplane, each recruited from every overrun town, and each hastily adorned with a painted white star, they rode and fought over two hundred miles in ten days.

On the 83rds flank was the huge 2nd Armored, with its tanks, artillery, self-propelled guns as well as bulldozers and armored cars. It was one of the largest and most powerful Divisions in Europe." The newspaper continued,

"Keeping up with the best of American armor just didn't belong in the books of modern warfare. It was impossible, but the 83rd Inf. Div. did it. They not only kept up with the armor — they outstripped it"

Actually, it was a tie race to the Elbe river. Within hours of one another, both Divisions secured a bridgehead across the river. However, the 2nd Div. was driven back and was obligated to cross the Elbe again with the 83rd on the bridge the Rag Tag Circus had entitled:

"Truman's Bridge — The Gateway To Berlin."

The 5th Armored had also reached the Elbe so here were three Generals with one thought in mind, be the first to reach Berlin! News of this sudden, unexpected advance went right up the line from General Simpson to General Bradley who took it to General Eisenhower. The bridgehead was now uppermost in everyone's mind. The ultimate goal, Berlin, was in sight of the Piper Cub spotter planes. There was no sign of any real German strength and the land was simply flat all the way to the capital of Germany.

No one could understand why we were suddenly told to 'Stand pat and wait for the Russians.' Truly we believed that General Ike had blown a golden opportunity. There was no doubt in anyone's mind, American troops could have made it to Berlin in a few days.

Most of us had become civilians before we learned the truth. When Bradley informed General Eisenhower of this sudden development he reportedly asked General Bradley his opinion on what the cost would be of breaking through and taking Berlin. Bradley's answer of "One hundred thousand men" ended the conversation.

Two days later, April 14th, Eisenhower cabled Washington his plans. In essence, he wanted to quickly destroy the German power in Denmark and the Danube valley. The Elbe bridgehead, while an unexpected opportunity, was covered in the Yalta Conference of 1943. Roosevelt and Churchill had agreed that all of this would be Russian territory.

There was no point in going any further at the cost of anymore lives. Rightfully so, "our race to Berlin" ended at the Elbe.

True military casualty figures on capturing Berlin varied. The official Russian figures stated 100,000 killed in the final assult of Berlin, which started at Oder, some twelve miles from the capital. Other reports from Marshall Zhukov were in the 150,000 range. General Bradley's orginal estimate of 100,000 was a total estimate of wounded and killed. Regardless, General Eisenhower's decision to make the Elbe river the Allied stopping point was a wise one.*

* Additional informative reading can be found in Cornelius Ryan's "The Last Battle" and John Keegan's "The Second World War."

★★★★

Chapter 18

Army Occupation

The war has ended and we're on the outskirts of Biere, a short distance from Magdeburg located on the Elbe river. As I stood with Wolf on the riverbank today, it was hard for us to realize that we had traveled this far from Normandy, to within fifty miles of Berlin, in eleven months. We are feeling high but the civilians aren't. They know the Russians have squatter's rights to the whole area. On May 11th we vacated the area moving back to Wofenbuttle at the base of the Hartz mountains. The living quarters are great because these are above average German homes.

My days are now spent with the gun inspection team. This allows some sightseeing time but all the towns are a horrible sight of total destruction. Sunday has been given back to us as a day of leisure. Our main conversations are still about "tickets home," the new point system. Rumors and Army news releases had our heads spinning. First you needed 100 points and now it has dropped to 80. — "Ginny, this system is not fair. We'd like 3 points for each month of combat, 2 for each month overseas and 1 for each month of service. As it stands now, a fellow stationed in England gets the same points as a fighting GI. Oh well, with my big total of 59 points I'm not going to lose any sleep over all the hell-ah-baloo. Things will change."

For some reason it took until May 15th before Lt.Gilham had to relinquish the pleasure of censoring my letters. I informed Ginny, "You can now ask anything." So, her first question was, "Tell me about the German girls." I replied,

"They resemble most of the girls in the other countries except they appear a little rounder on the bottom."

We are getting many passes to the hospital town of Bad Harzbarg and the place is loaded with German nurses. We quickly noticed their bottoms weren't all that round. It's still a strict 'no, no' to talk to any German. I observed many fellows getting severe eye strain as they sat on the stone walls by the sidewalk. They were emitting odd guttural sounds. It's not a healthy condition.

"It's May 23 and Lt. Gilman has orientated us with our relationship to the Pacific war. He gave us our four official probabilities.

> 1. Army of Occupation here
> 2. Pacific Bound (by Suez Canal or U.S.)
> 3. Breakup of Division
> 4. Return to the States

The Lt. is leaning toward the first two, but I've seen him wrong before! It's another wait and see job. The Pacific war is far from over. The last thing any of us want to do is get retrained to go to that hot war zone."

Ginny wrote me the good news that Ed Perry has been found in a prison camp. He has been through hell. As he was dropping, the Germans shot and broke his leg. Later on he caught pneumonia and on a forced march he almost died. The news that my first Army bed partner was on his way home was good to hear. It made my day.

Somehow Charlie Rohrer talked Sgt. Jones into letting him borrow a Jeep to go visit his best, hometown friend. I was invitied to go along for this dandy change of pace.

The use of headlights was still not allowed, so we had to be sure to allow enough time to come the 125 miles back on the super highway. We had our fill of cat eye driving.

"Ginny, Charlie was just cruising along when we came upon a strange convoy of six foreign cars painted with large, white U.S. stars. As we slowly passed them, we took notice that in each rear seat there sat a high ranking officer. Charlie expressed some concern about passing them but I proclaimed, 'Nothing to fear; you're under the 45 M.P.H. speed limit.' With that said the second car pulled out and came up alongside us. A Captain with glistening eyes and a pointing finger pulled us over. He spoke.

'Where in the hell is the fire?' Charlie, in his best military manner replied;

'Sir, we're obeying the 45 mile speed limit.'

'Soldier, for you, the speed limit is 35!' Without the blink of an eye the Captain left us in his dust. We sat there looking at one another, then we burst out laughing while I managed;

'This is a fine thing you got us into, Ollie. Now how are we going to beat the sunset home?'

Charlie replied, 'It's your turn to drive.'

After a bit, suddenly things changed. The convoy was coming back to us! This highway had many bomb craters and here was a long stretch of filled in craters. With their delicate cargo the convoy had slowed to a crawl. I maintained a speed that just managed to keep our rugged bodies in the Jeep. Charlie was concerned.

'Rags, this isn't going to work.' How right he was. Again the Captain quickly came out and pulled us over. I whispered to Charlie that the Captain's ears looked redder. He didn't waste any words.

'Your speed limit is now 25!' Now Charlie turned on me, 'Well, Laurel, this is a fine mess you got us into.'

We barely kept them in view for the next 15 miles. Then they suddenly turned off. I floored her and hit sixty as the detour sign came into view. I convinced Charlie the road couldn't be bad enough to stop a new, four wheeled Jeep. Zooming another mile we noticed we were climbing and sure enough — a huge blown out bridge. This was not a defeat. Back we tore to find a place to go over the side and through the woods. We lucked out. The woods were not too thick but what a ride it was. From the woods we startled a farmer at his barn. After wading a creek we ground our way up a steep bank. Climbing the last hill we were all smiles. This was a victory for the little guys.

As we rounded a long curve an unbelievable sight caught our eyes. That convoy was just turning onto the highway! This was another bombed area and it was now dusk. With raised eyebrows we looked at one another. Would that mean Captain be expecting to see Laurel and Hardy again? We had to give it the old Army try. Slowly I eased the Jeep by as Charlie mumbled something about the brig. Getting past I glued my eyeballs on the rear view mirror. All the cars had turned on their small headlights. Thankfully, everyone was staying in line. The highway was taking us on a long, steep climb. Slowly but surely I increased our speed and, as soon as I went over the top, I floored the Jeep. Charlie hollered, 'Here he comes!' There was no turning back now. The race was on. Just one question remained. Could a new Jeep go faster than an unknown foreign car?

The first five miles were exciting. It was up hill and down dale and through bomb craters. They were showing more speed on the straight away, but we had the advantage on the hills and the craters. With just fifteen miles to go, we relaxed and enjoyed our cat and mouse game.

On reaching the Wolfenbuttel exit the Captain's lights were barely visible. Turning our lights off we disappeared into the city. We didn't need to tell one another that our smiles mirrored those of Laurel and Hardy.

The next morning Charlie and I were still smiling when Sgt. Jones called us to his office.

'Where the hell did you guys have that Jeep?'

'On the autobahn, Sarge!' Charlie replied.

'Since when is that a mucky road covered with under-brush? God damn it, you go look under that Jeep and then you come back here and tell me what you guys were up to!'

Boy, were we dumb. There was a whole mess of bushes underneath the Jeep and it was loaded with mud. It really was a terrible mess. I turned to Charlie and said, 'I'm only a Sgt., Ollie, you better do the explaining.' Charlie told the truth, 'There was a slight detour which took us through some woods and a——' Jones interrupted. 'Sure, sure and the cheese is damn green on the moon. Get your butts out of here and I want to see that Jeep spotless.'"

****

As Memorial Day drew near, we were working every day doing extensive overhauls on every howitzer. At night the Company had close order drills for an hour preparing for the Memorial Day ceremony. The honoring of fallen comrades became a very moving experience. There were not many dry eyes around when the playing of taps echoed off the Hartz mountains in Bad Harzburg.

Frustration was the word for the discharge point system. "Ginny, an outfit of ninety men have moved in next to us. They're back from a thirty day leave in the United States. The ship broke down in New York so they got thirty more. They all have over 100 points!! Tomorrow they're supposed to pack for home again. So please don't believe what you're reading about armies coming home. In the past year we have changed armies eleven times. You just hang in there."

Be aware all is not gloom. Tonight we had 22 gallons of ice cream for our shrinking company of 80 men. The Germans make it for thirty cents a gallon after we supply all the ingredients. It's actually not costing us a cent. In the course of events we had come across stacks of useless 1923 money. The Germans love it.

D Day, plus a year, was a day of partying. The thoughts were expressed that time seemed to be condensed because so much has happened in these twelve months. Doggett also returned from a free Riviera trip.

"Dog's $35 a day room and all his meals were free, but he still spent $300 on partying. He's so wound up we can't shut him up. 'The MPs will only pick you up for murder. The town is off limits to officers, which means there are no murders!' Dog is one of a kind.

The Russians are moving in all around us which tells us we'll soon be pulling up stakes. Our destination is known, but for unknown reasons, I'm not to tell. I'm hoping this is the last move before the 'Good Ship Lollipop.'"

****

In two days of convoy we covered 410 miles. We are set up outside Passau on the bank of the blue Danube. It's June 11th and we're replacing the 5th Div., which was the first division to come overseas and the 12th to land in Normandy.

Our mental state took another blow when they informed us we were headed for the Pacific. The resistance on Okinawa has just ended at the cost of 10,000 men with another 5000 wounded. "Ginny, these figures convince me we should stay off Japan. The safest way is to bomb and starve them into submission.

Our new quarters are adequate. It's a two-story building next to a modern factory large enough to house all our vehicles. We're almost back to basics. Our working day is 8:15 to 5:00 with an hour for lunch. Wednesdays and Saturdays are half days. The free afternoons require us to participate in a sport. I'm starting to trot along the river, and I'm playing centerfield on our ball team.

Bond and I have the tedious task of inspecting, cleaning and repairing hundreds of binoculars. It's a slow, boring job. In a sense we're feeling like Army civilians, but I'm not complaining. We're once again under Patton's command and the rest of the Division is doing basic drilling, hiking and standing reveille and retreat. I'm counting my blessings and holding my breath.

The needed discharge points are now 85. Dog and Bond qualify, but for some reason they are lost in the shuffle. As our top point men leave, the commander is filling the spots with all kinds of top noncoms. This has made us and a number of Companies top heavy. New orders arrived today requiring rank for rank transfers. For everyone, this whole system is mass confusion. Our living quarters are nicknamed 'Binocular Row.' We soon discovered a bathing beach right across the river in Austria. And Wolf was quickly aware that the Austrian girl had a unique method of changing into her bathing suit while still keeping on her dress. I believe their gyrations have created a new dance step. This is a fine time to run out of movie film. Every warm lunch hour all riverside windows have at least one set of protruding binoculars."

****

"Patton's long arm has caught us. Saturday morning inspections are back; all stripes have to be on every piece of uniform which drew Dog to comment, 'Hell, Rags, after three years I think I know who you are!' The worst regulation requires us to carry a firearm everytime we go off the base. For sure it's time for Patton to go home.

Last evening, as a Sgt., I was pulling Pvt. of the Guard. It was 5 a.m. I was sitting in a military manner digesting the Reader's Digest. On hearing someone whistling a happy tune my ears went on military alert. Next my eyes were popped wide open. A tall blonde figure was approaching in tight fitting slacks. Her well spoken English greeting sent goose bumps down my spine. 'Hi, I've been looking for you all night.' I didn't fall for that line; I knew she wanted oil for her truck. I woke the Sgt. of the Guard who woke the automotive Sgt. They both agreed that I was to send her to the military government in Passau. This was before they met her! As the Sgt.s went to get her oil, she started to question me on which cities the Russians controlled. My left eyebrow started to quiver, so I proceeded to the back of her truck to check its cargo. Raising the tarp my eyes made out the huddled, cramped figures of old women and small children. Our good deed for the day was completed before sunrise."

June the 18th I was writing, "The Division's classification has been changed to Number 2, which means 'to the Pacific.!' It's been expected. Right now it doesn't concern me so don't fret. It won't occur soon. It could mean a furlough in the States at Christmas.

Lt. Gilman is getting back at me for all the letters I made him censor. He's sending me for a week of schooling in Regensburg ninety miles up the road. This is the same course he took that caused us that long Jeep ride back to Liege. You'll die laughing at the title, 'How To Teach Teachers To Teach.' The two of us are supposedly going to teach our Sgt.'s teachers methods on dealing with occupational troops. Oh yes, we're still going to the Pacific. If your Dad can figure this out, let me know."

****

The school was interesting and different. In the class of twelve there were ten officers, a 5 stripe Sgt. and me. I sat on the edge of my seat waiting for someone to shout, "Rangnow, you're on guard!"

I had a private room in the hotel and all meals were served on real plates with linen napkins. Classes ran all the way from ten to noon. In the afternoons I went to the college track to prepare for the 4th of July Division meet. The German 400 meter track seemed a lot longer than the old Olney High one.

Because of rain, the meet was held on July 8th before hundreds of interested civilians. It was my lucky day. From the starter's hat I picked the pole position. His gun went off and I jumped out like a young hare. In no time at all we were around the last turn and I was still in front. Then suddenly there appeared a whole mess of fellows in front of me. I hollered at my legs to go get them but their pounding feet drowned out my cry of despair. As I sputtered across the finish line, I was happy to see three guys behind me. I told Ginny, "My legs need some practice running between the Pennsy station and the subway. Anyway, it felt good to run again and learn that I was still fast enough to catch girls."

Sgt. Jones and Master Sgt. Downing left us today and were replaced with a T/5 and P.F.C.. There are still 26 guys here with over 85 points. The Captain can't find any proper replacements. Major Smith became our new Colonel and immediately acted like Patton. "No Sgt.s will be allowed to eat at the same table with a T/5 or Pvt." The crazy Army is back.

Our off and on again Pacific war is back on again. The 83rd has turned this area over to the 102nd. Some of us will be starting Pacific training in the mountains of Germany.

Wolf said, "Come on, Rags, this farmer is going to teach you how to fish the Danube." As he laughed, I followed this stringless fisherman to the river. Displaying his Ohio grin, he pulled out three hand grenades.

When the fraternization ban was lifted the people at home quickly expressed some concern. I told Ginny. "The policy wasn't working well. It added a lot of confusion in our everyday dealings of trying to reorganize the country. There will be girl problems, but we will have to deal with these people a lot longer than the troops of 1918."

July 14, 1945
Here are some facts from the 83rd's book, 'Thunderbolt Across Europe,' which should interest you and the General. It gives our whole battle history. I will be mailing it when I can wrap it properly. Here are a few interesting statistics. Bear in mind, in Atterbury, we started out with 15,000 men.

Casualties

Killed in action 2,850
Died of wounds 425
Total 3,275
Seriously wounded 3,809
Slightly wounded 6,096
Seriously injured 111
Slightly injured 1,044
Total 11,060
Captured 177
Missing in action 501
Total 678

Total Battle Casualties 15,013

Enemy Equipment Destroyed

Tanks 480
Airplanes 61
Supply trains 29
Artillery pieces 969

Miscellaneous

Days of contact with enemy 270
Prisoners captured 82,146
Rounds of artillery fired 410,251
Rounds small arms, mortars 21,899,868
Miles of field wire layed 11,868

Company wise, Doc Pfeifer's automotive crew repaired 2,389 vehicles. In Normandy they installed 700 wire cutters on various vehicles. Singlehandedly Lloyd Grayson repaired 711 radiators. Ambrey and Unfried fixed 1,238 carburetors, 202 generators, 177 fuel pumps and 900 batteries.

Sgt. Harris's crew fixed 14,995 small arms and reclaimed 18,548 from the battlefield. Gene and I got honorable mention for repairing 632 various instruments and evacuating another 1,113 to the rear, which were mainly watches.

****

With the ending of the fraternization ban the male sex drive came to the fore. Every friendly German girl became pretty. Right across our back lot there is a big, striking blonde. Our big automotive guy soon won her over. He was in heaven. Early last night he came storming in heading for the bathroom. Wolf came out laughing informing us our lover boy was furiously washing his face and brushing his teeth. The story was they were having a great kissing bout when she went oral. Suddenly he saw visions of many German soldiers doing the same thing. He hopped out of bed, jumped into his pants and ran home. This morning Wolf informed the Lt., "We don't need anymore sex films; we have the girl next door.

"The Division Newspaper headlines of July 30th read,

'The 83rd Will Finish Pacific Training By Sept.17th.' To confuse matters we turned in our gas masks plus the size of long johns and winter overcoats. They requested the destination of our furlough. That sounds like good Christmas cheer, but the bad news is six of us are leaving to start Pacific maneuvers. It's a 200 mile trip up in the German mountains. There's no doubt, the long arm of the Pacific is tapping us on the shoulder.

****

"Another terrible experience. Here I was all snuggled in bed when this horrible noise sounded, a BUGLE! It just doesn't seem possible, but I am writing from a tent housing fourteen other fellows. We're attached to the Headquarters Company of Division Artillery. However, once again we are lucky. As I write this, all the other troops are standing inspection before standing retreat.

This is an interesting camp because the woods are loaded with all types of German aircraft in various stages of assembly. Today's Stars and Stripes is also amazing. It states it will cost us 268,000 dead and wounded to take Japan's first island. That would be a senseless price to pay. Now, don't fret your head over these type of articles. I can't see how this Division can be retrained and sent that far before the invasion. No, I'm not making any ice cream bets on this one."

****

Aug. 7, 1945

"What an odd feeling this morning, hearing the artillery fire round after round. Graham and I watched one crew fire their first round. It fell a hundred yards short. If they keep that up, we'll never qualify for Japan.

What has surprised us is the weather. It's so darn cold our teeth were chattering double time until ten a.m. We'd make lousy Scouts. We're not prepared for this change.

Ginny, we had a great surprise visit today from one Art Doggett. He came all the way up here just to deliver your letters. Then he had to rub it in by informing us that the 783rd now has its own night club in Austria. For your benefit Dog then added, 'All the girls are fat.'"

August the 8th was just another cold, rainy day. As Graham and I were walking between gun positions, we noticed four fellows standing in a circle. One was doing all the talking with a great amount of arm waving. Before we got to them he was off and running to another group. Graham commented, "Now, there's a guy who just got his shipping orders." On reaching the first group one of the fellows turned and asked, "Did you hear the news? We dropped a big bomb on Japan and it blew up the whole city!" Our odd look brought the added comment, "It was an atomic bomb!" This didn't make any sense either, but it was apparent something big had happened. Rushing to our radio we soon grasped the meaning of the bomb and we too started waving our arms.

For the rest of the day and up to till midnight we sat on Wolf's cot listening to his radio while discussing everything from Einstein to the bomb's effect on us and future wars. "This has to shorten the war." "I wonder how many of these things we have." "Hey, maybe now we'll just head for home." "This is really horrible, one bomb killing one hundred thousand people." "Maybe Buck Rodgers isn't too far away after all." As the night wore on the thinking got a little deeper. "This is the start of an unlimited source of power." "More than anything it means the world must find a way for lasting peace."

The next day the rain washed us right out of our tent. As we huddled in the small arms truck, heating it with a blow torch, the radio announced a second bomb had been dropped. Wolf shouted, "This war can be over in a month!"

As darkness fell, the storm reached gale proportions. Dog was trying to sing with a Glen Miller song when they broke in, "Here is a bulletin from..." There was a loud crash as a huge tree took out our generator. The winds were howling and a thunderous downpour was plummeting the tent. Dog was now moaning, "Oh laudie me." It was a scary, long, cold night. I wrote Ginny, "This morning I was all worn out from running in bed all night. There was a river running through the tent and Wolf was shouting, 'I'm not moving without a life jacket.'"

The weekend found us back in Passau. "The changes in the Company are amazing. Civilians are doing most of the kitchen work. The chow line has been replaced by family style serving on real plates. I found the night club interesting. Plump Hungarian girls were trying to learn jitterbugging. Wolf was concerned about the floors stress factor.

The rumor mills are going full blast. Everyone is excited over the possibility that the war is over, but there haven't been any premature celebrations.

Also today, of all things, I visited Bond in the hospital. This is a sad state of affairs. He caught his finger in the grinder. Now he is afraid of being left behind when Dog and the other high pointers leave."

****

"Here we are back in the mountains and all dressed up to welcome Patton. He just flew over, but it was too foggy to land. Wolf's comment, 'Darn, I'm disappointed. Back on the farm I could have gotten ten bucks for his autograph.'

****

"This is August 14th. We're listening to the people in New York celebrating the wars end. We're just sitting, waiting. This has been so drawn out I doubt if we do much celebrating. At least our General is alert. He has called in all ammunition."

It was eight the next morning when the long awaited news reached us. As for celebrating, there wasn't any. The pouring rain put a damper on everything. Wolf quipped, "If this keeps up, they'll be able to dock our ship in this tent." The rain stopped long enough in the afternoon for the General to give us a pep talk. 'I'm hoping the maneuvers will soon be called off, but you know the Army and you're still in the Army.'"

His hope came true three days later and we happily returned to Passau. New orders and rumors came out daily. The needed points were now down to 75. This made me eligible with a million other guys. I wasn't impressed.

"We have started our own Company newspaper and I have the honor of writing a sports column. All kinds of vocational courses are being taught, and Lt. Gilman is still trying to get even with me. On fifteen minutes notice he asked me to teach his class. When I raised my right eyebrow he gave me his big grin, 'Heck, Rags, I'll lend you my notes!'"

****

"Here it is the end of August and Bond is still in the hospital. It was a going away party last night for the 16 old timers. Naturally I ended up putting sad sack Doggett to bed. I knew he would never remember my last hug so I got up at six this morning to see them off. As I waved my last so long to Charlie Rohrer and Earl Graham, I realized the 783rd was changed forever.

Today we received the news that the 83rd is now part of the Occupational Army. This means we high pointers will some day be shipped to another outfit returning to the States. No ice cream bets."

This time the Army moved fast. On Sept. 2nd I sent Ginny a puzzle. "Can you imagine watching a group of grown men passing around their little black books. Nope, they are not collecting hot numbers. Can you believe we're swapping home addresses? Hold it now, I'm not headed for the Good Ship Lollipop. You won't believe this, but, yes, you will, we're headed in the opposite direction. Would you believe — Czechoslovakia?

Next week 6,500 of us are headed for Pilsen to join the 8th Armd. Div. We will pack them up for shipment to the States. I'm hoping I don't have to ride home in a tank but, if I find one that floats, I'll be on my way.

All our officers are staying here to keep a semblance of order. Of the orginal 783rd Company only four are staying. They are one point shy of the magic number."

****

"It was a farewell party at the club tonight and this party equated to your Navy's affairs. Everything was flowing and it was free. With tears running down his face the band leader gave a heart tugging speech remarking what a great bunch of men we are. Then he played a nice song that he had written for us, which drew a cheer and a great round of applause.

Suddenly the reality of these events seem like strange, virgin territory. The 83rd and the 783rd are almost gone. The finish line is almost in sight; our Army careers are over. Now listen, Ginny, I'll be sprinting rather fast coming down your sidewalk, so please, sort of stand aside and just extend your hand."

The next day we gave a little shout on hearing the peace treaty was signed on the battleship Missouri. There was also a trip to the hospital for a last "Goodbye" with Gene Bond. It's a sad situation. He is now waiting for an operation in a French hospital. Why they haven't shipped him to the States is a mystery to everyone.

"Here it is Sept. 7 and it will be your last letter from Germany. The train leaves at 4 a.m. We'll be joining the 8th's Ordnance with the task of packing all the rifles in cases. Wolf quipped,

'Ragsy, you're going to learn to work like a farmer.'

Late this afternoon I found Lt. Gilman and we said our farewells. After a hardy handshake, he wished me well but then added he felt sorry for you. He did not choose to explain, but he wondered aloud how long Burholme would have to wait for a wedding to take place. I can't understand his sudden interest in our neighborhood weddings. At least I left him grinning. It's been a pleasure knowing and working with the good Lieutenant.

Now I must get to work on the problem of how to pack and carry all this stuff to Czechoslovakia. Isn't it amazing; here's a new language and already I can spell a fourteen letter word. See you in the next country."

Chapter 19

The Long Way Home

The trip to Czechoslovakia made me feel like I had taken a journey back in time. The train consisted of fourteen old World War I cars called 40 by 8s. That was their size. We had twenty to a car. This provided just enough space so we could all lay down at the same time.

For the first couple of hours we stopped at every town to hook up a few more cars then watch the crying girls wave goodbye. By late afternoon we were up to fifty crawling cars. The night can best be described as a jerky, groaning and moaning, sleepless night. As I slowly focused my eyes in the morning, I realized I was looking at the most primitive land of the eight nations we had visited. There wasn't a single paved road outside the towns. Many men and women were working in the fields. As we slowly passed they would straighten up and wave. Some of the men were throwing their hands up into the sky in apparent disbelief. We crazy Americans were supposed to be going home, not east!

Our arrival was timed to the 8th Division's high pointers departure. As we pulled into the Pilsen station, nine hours late, we were greeted with another funny sight. Many of the departing soldiers were carrying flowers which they had received by yet another group of crying girls. Wolf commented,

"Boy, the florists around here have a good thing going."

While the surrounding area looks ancient our quarters are a modern gym. The 783rd has been broken up into small pieces but Wolf and I have a private room. Musser is around the corner. Our view overlooks the gym floor on which just girls work out. They range from tots to upper teenagers. This made Wolf ask, "Ragsy, did you keep any binoculars?"

****

"From the looks of things our shipping date will be late October. A move of this scale has to create mass confusion.

Yesterday Musser and I started the sore finger job of unloading 9,000 ammunition clips. This is just the tip of an iceberg. But the town is exciting. As Wolf and I ambled down main street we were stopped in our tracks. Twenty guys on horseback were galloping at us like we were on the wrong end of a Hollywood western. The men were wearing many different styles of uniforms and of various colors. Each shouting horseman had a chest full of medals.

'My God,' Wolf exclaimed, 'it's the Russians again!' I added, 'Now tell me Les, how did these guys ever beat the Germans?'

You know this is the messed up part of Czechoslovakia. In the first World War it was German territory and then given back. Some Germans stayed and in this war they were loyal to Germany. Now they must wear arm bands and be off the street by 9:30 p.m. This history we learned the hard way. The three of us were walking down main street to our first breakfast. We smiled and nodded a 'good morgan' to the passing civilians. We were appalled when they completely ignored us. Wolf shot me a glance. 'Ragsy, you need a bath.'

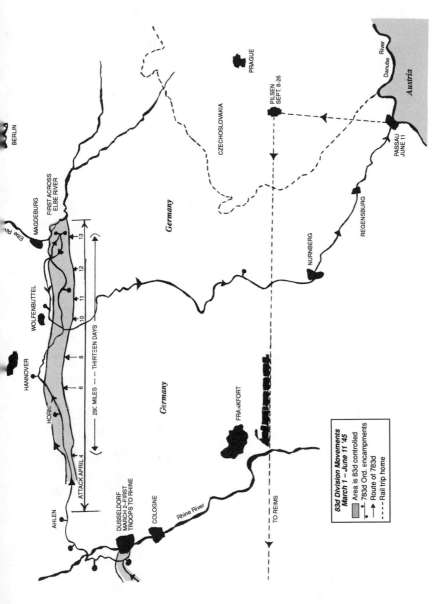

Division Moves — March 1 to June 11, 1945

At breakfast we were informed on the facts of life. The Czecks weren't speaking to any Americans because some dumb GIs were bringing German girls to Czech run dances. I can understand their feelings, but I don't like this bit of being ignored on the streets.

'Peaches, (Wolf's love letter name) I want out of here.'

'Don't matter, Ragsy, you still need a bath.'"

****

"Things were looking up today. A ten year old boy stopped by our room. He was trying to sell his sister. Wolf took the lad by surprise.

'We're not interested in your sister's undies but hows chances of getting our's washed?' The handsome boy quickly agreed. In a flash he was off with a full barracks bag of our clothes. I crossed my fingers that we would see him again. Four hours later he did return. As he received his pay his face broke into a great grin. It cost us a packet of four cigarettes, two oranges and a Milky Way bar. It wasn't like we cheated him. On the Czech market a carton of cigarettes is bringing forty dollars."

The following six days we loaded freight cars from early morning till late in the evening. Most of our dinners were missed, but we had an ample supply of candy bars. Our mission was clear. "When the Division is packed you go home!"

Leadership was a problem and Ginny got the whole story. "Musser and I practically had 8,000 rifles packed in this freight car when our new Colonel comes along and says,

'Soldier, that's not the way I was taught.' Out came the rifles to be repacked his way. I thought soft spoken Musser would never stop cussin so I said, 'Muss, we must be close to getting out. We sweated when we came in so I guess they won't less us out until we sweat again.'

****

Ginny's asking me the serious questions of what am I going to do as a civilian. "That's a good question for many of us but the GI Bill sounds like a good program for further education. Right now I simply lay on my cot at night and wonder what it's going to feel like to be home again."

****

"Our hard work has paid off. You can put your worn out pen on the shelf. We're taking the train to France and our boat is scheduled for Sept. 30th.! They are telling us we should be out in six weeks. The three of us have been romping around this gym like three little kids in a toy store."

Chapter 20

France — Again

Our high spirits of heading home were soon broken by the 40 and 8 train ride. Our car was whipping like a snake's tail and at first it was humorous but, as the hours dragged by, anger set in. It became impossible to sleep. We were rolling all over the car and into one another.

Musser shouted, "This is a nightmare, that's what it is; it's a damn nightmare!"

Finally at six a.m. the train halted. Muss and I hopped off and ran to the cars coupler. Grunting and groaning we struggled with mechanical might. When the train started the car ran straight. We were instant heroes. For a reward we received an extra pile of straw.

Everytime we crossed a country border we lost the steam engine. The first day it happened twice. We sat for a total of seven hours. With limited toilet facilities (passing trees) it was quite a sight when the train stopped. Meals were so few and far between we resorted to K rations.

If our long train stopped near a village, it was instantly mobbed by civilians who were eager to buy anything offered. Many GIs were ready to sell — anything! Army blankets brought $10.00, a dollar for a bar of soap and nickel candy bars were worth fifty cents. Wolf observed the scene and then spoke his words of wisdom.

"The aftermath of war, Rags, is also a hell of a sight."

On day five the train rumbled through Reims to our new home just south of Paris. It was a huge tent city called Camp Oklahoma.

Picking up my worn out pen I wrote, "The administration, mess halls and movies are the only permanent buildings. We have no formations or exercises. There are no duties to perform. KP is handled by prisoners of war which caused Wolf to ask, 'Who's testing the food?'

It feels like recruit time again. Our days have been spent standing in lines for shots, clothing, signing many papers and exchanging money. After signing one which stated I had no knowledge of war crimes Wolf chided me.

'You're lying, the crime we're in now can't get any bigger.'

The last line of the day was a real surprise. The French Government paid us $17.50 for services rendered. I'll put it towards your Christmas gift, hoping you get it this year. Our ship and shipping date have been sunk. Now we are supposed to move to Camp Lucky Strike and then sail from jolly old England. Try to stay calm!"

****

Ten days have passed and there's no doubt that we are stuck in the old Army game of hurry up and wait. It has done nothing but rain and, again, the mud is everywhere. Eating is the biggest highlight of the day. But this standing in a chow and movie line for twenty minutes in these French downpours is washing us out.

Thankfully, Ginny disobeyed me and continued to write. She excitedly told of her brother Chis's and Ed Perry's homecoming. Her daily "up" letters helped me to stay on an even keel with all our daily, maddening changes.

On visiting Reims I sent Ginny a telegram which caused the clerk to raise his left eyebrow.

"Detained Indefinitely. Please Rush Washtub and Paddle."

Every day was the same. I'd play table tennis in the morning and afternoon. In the evening it was a movie or a letter explaining our latest snafu.

"It's October 2nd and supposedly we're moving to Camp Lucky Strike on the 8th. Shortly after, on the 20th, it will be up the gangplank. Bite another nail."

Three days later the tune was, "By golly, the radio just announced that me and Wolf are on the high seas. Let's hope you didn't read that. The Top Sgt. tried to make amends. He gathered us all together and said we will now be transferred to Lucky Strike on the 16th. Three days later we will move to Camp Phillip Morris. This was too much for Wolf. Holding up one finger he spoke.

'I get it now. We have to collect every brand of cigarette before we get our boat ride home.'"

The magic day came and went. Now it was the Captain's turn to confuse us. "I want you fellows to stop passing around all these rumors because they're all true." As I shook my head to clear it, the Captain went on. "Now get back in your tents and pack; we're moving today!"

Two days later I wrote, "We've been sitting on our packs all day and the only change is a sad one. We just said our goodbye to Vin Musser. His 70 points got him moved to a lower camp. A letter from Bond didn't help. Not only was his operation a failure, but he is still in France and he has no idea of his future.

****

The Captain was one-third right. We moved but it was the wrong day and the wrong camp. This is the 13th and the camp is Chicago. The name brought a smile to Wolf's face and he explained, "Chicago sounds closer to home." His smile left when they moved him down the road. Naturally we'd like to board the same ship this year.

During the next week Wolf moved three times ending up in the next tent. Then we heard the British had reclaimed the Queen liners so I advised Ginny, "Send the darn washtub."

"Passes to Paris are available every day but too many GI, tipsy drivers were leaving the highways. I opted for Reims where I read a U.S.O. notice.

"French man wants to meet American soldier."

An elderly woman took my application asking the usual: name, rank and serial number. Then she asked the name of my unknown Company Commander. When I shrugged, she frowned.

"You Americans!"

A young French girl guided me to my new friend, Jacques Macquart. He is 32 and a professor of art at the Reims college. He and his Mom share an adequate apartment. There was a language difficulty, but our two meetings were an educational experience. Jacques gave me a ringside seat of what it was like living under the Nazis.

The last visit was embarrassing. They sat me down to a full French dinner. He told me his monthly salary was $82.00 and I knew that I was eating a half a month of that. The whole meal was purchased off the black market. These were fine people and we promised to stay in touch.

On the windy afternoon of November 8th it was, "For sure you are moving on November 12th to Camp Phillip Morris where you will get your shipping date." That night I awoke with a painful sore shoulder. As I sought a new position, I realized my left index finger was beating its own tango. I sat straight up as I remembered knicking it playing table tennis — last week!

Blood poisoning! I'd get murdered if I turned on the lights. I hopped in my boots and went out under the street lamp. There were no stripes but the darn thing really hurt. I thought of Bond, then the boat, then I marched over to the medics and awoke the sleepy medic. He agreed it seemed like a strange gland reaction. He gave me two aspirins, patted me on the back and said, "You'll be okay." As soon as my head hit the cot, I broke out with chills and sweats. By dawn's early light I was a true sad sack.

At sick call they took one look at the thermometer, then pointed the way to the ambulance. On my second day I was still feeling lousy. A new nurse gently held my finger and listened to my tale of woe.

"Forget the finger; I'm making you a new man by morning." She handed me a can of juice with four large pills. Those pills ran the old man right out of me and down the drain.

The Captain smiled, "I'll sign you out tomorrow." Two hours later two fellows I hardly knew, came to tell me we were leaving tomorrow! I searched the hospital for the Captain. Finally I found him and, with a big grin, he signed me out on the spot.

As I checked the bulletin board back in the barracks, I couldn't believe my eyes.

"All men will be ready to leave at 0200, November 13. You will board a train in Laon to be transported to the sea port of Marseille."

Wolf had just returned. He read it, then gave his view.

"It's all perfectly clear. Already they're starting this educational bill. We didn't have to sign up. They're training us to become American hobos."

Of course, it was a day late when we left, but we did arrive at the railroad siding at two in the morning. It was raining. It took another two hours before the powers that be noticed we were soaked. We were moved under shelter where we stayed until 1:00 the next afternoon.

When we finally got the order, "Go to your assigned cars," lo and behold, a loud Lt. claimed it was his car. He ordered us to sit on the bank. A half hour later a Captain asked, "Why the hell are you guys sitting here?" In short order he had us a car. It wasn't a 40 by 8, but it didn't have any glass in the front door. It was a cold wind that blew through that door as we huddled on the wooden benches for another miserable, long night.

It was a K ration breakfast with a promise of a hot meal at four. We got the meal that night at 10:30, but it was worth the wait. The tired mess guys were jolly and the food was hot. They fed 1,000 of us in thirty-five minutes.

Two of our fellows were on the ball. They rushed back from chow and "borrowed" a wooden fence. After sealing up the door, they made makeshift bunks on the luggage racks. Wolf and I ended up on the floor where the aisle was so narrow it was necessary to sleep on your side. At least we were warm.

We traveled 120 miles during the night and the second day was all stop and go. Everyone was grumpy until they told us we were 150 miles from port and 10 miles from a hot meal. The meal came four hours later while the last leg took another sixteen hours. We were all in agreement. For a complete Army experience, every soldier should have to take a train ride in the European Theatre of Operations.

On November 19th I wrote Ginny. "This camp is a bit different. It has sandy soil and they have terrific winds causing small sand storms. Tents came down last night and the darn stuff sweeps into everything. To survive we all slept under the blankets.

Here, too, all is confusion. Can you believe they processed us again? The same long lines and the same old questions. Our hopes soared Tuesday when we were assigned to the "David Farragut" and told to stay in our tents. Friday we were still there and the Stars and Stripes told us it had sailed on Thursday. So the Captain called us out and said, 'Keep faith, the Farragut hasn't docked yet.'" Twenty yards behind me I could hear another Captain telling his troops, 'The Farragut has sailed with French troops."

This was a bit much. Last night some of the fellows started chanting, 'We want to go home.' It picked up from tent to tent until the whole camp was in an uproar. Today the Post Commander got smart. He ordered the PXs to turn off all the beer.

The short ride to the Marseilles' docks came on Monday, November 27th. In my last letter to Ginny I said, "Our spirits are soaring. I promise I'll be home to hang up your Christmas stocking. This is an ice cream bet."

Chapter 21

The
"Good Ship Lollipop"

Every neck was straining to catch the first glimpse of "Our" ship. And suddenly there she was, a good old Liberty freighter. To me it looked like the Queen Mary. Wolf was glad to see it didn't have a row of protruding oars.

Within the hour we had bunked down and exchanged our Francs for that good looking American money. Wolf and I stood side by side. We had made it, and there wasn't another 83rd man on board.

Our ship is the Sea Ashe and she is 440 feet long and 56 feet wide. She can hold 330 freight cars but, with a cargo of just 550 anxious soldiers, she is empty. We have plenty of room to move around but our sleeping quarters leave a lot to be desired. The two sleeping compartments are fifty foot square with bunks piled six feet high. They are made of tight strung canvas and they rise in pairs. Wolf is on my left, six inches away, while the fellow on the right is two feet. To prevent breathing on one another we sleep head to toe. Wolf had to comment on this. "Ragsy, could I try smelling your nose?"

Fellows assigned to the top bunks are subjected to a tough climb plus constant horseplay of leg grabbing and being goosed. This room is too hot and it has the smell that only a hulk full of men can have. I'm spending as much time on deck as the weather allows.

The first meal was great, hot boiled ham and American ice cream. It was our first in 21 months. As we went on deck for the first time, we caught a beautiful sunset on a mirror like Mediterranean. The train rides were forgotten.

This morning we stripped to the waist and layed on the hatch watching the coast of Spain drifting by. Wolfe spoke.

"Wouldn't it be something if we walk into our homes, right in the middle of a snowstorm, with a full sun tan?"

This is an Army dream cruise. We have no duties; we're simply uniform-clad passengers. Our one gripe is the slowness of the Sea Ashe. Her top speed is 11 knots. On hearing this Wolfe had a suggestion.

"Let's break out the oars and take turns rowing." By using simple math, 11 knots, 24 hours a day equals 264 miles a day or about 11 days to the States. That means we'll be docking around the 10th. A little slow, but that's plenty of time before Christmas.

On telling Wolf that we should get up at six tomorrow and see the Rock of Gibraltar, he replied,

"Rags, that's just a rock. There' nothing there to excite an old Ohio farm boy."

I got up and watched solo. By midmorning the winds had kicked up the ocean and the Ashe was bobbing like a nibble on a cork line. Many guys are green and hanging over the railing while others have sought their cots for relief. Wolf and I were needling one another about getting green around the gills. It wasn't going to happen to me, especially in front of a farm boy.

For lunch we had a nice, chicken dinner sitting on our favorite, middle hatch. With his familiar grin Wolf said,

"Ragsy, you better find a place at the rail." I was swallowing hard but it didn't help. I lost my chicken dinner.

The third night a fierce lightning storm kept us below deck. In my journal I wrote, "The crew maintains a large map, inking in a line which shows our location and the 24 hour mileage. Yesterday we made 250 miles so we're right on target. Our daily routine is now set at reading, some cards and hoping for a good evening movie. However, the weather and our daily mileage is the main topic of conversation and the ship is loaded with experts.

The next day seemed calm, but the ship was still bobbing like a cork. I questioned a crewman and he said,

"You guys are our ballast, so with no weight, the ship is riding high."

Wolf and I had to check this out. Leaning over the stern we got shocked. Not only was the ship floating way above the water line, but one-third of the prop was out of the water. As Wolf looked at his watch, I counted the prop's revolutions. When I announced "60" Wolf declared,

"That does it, let's get out the oars."

The excitement today was a sick soldier. They transferred him to a faster ship. As we were watching this risky, rope and pulley transfer, old Wolf suggested maybe we ought to fake an illness.

"Peaches, with our luck we'd either fall in or the ship would be headed for France."

This December 4 is one scary day. The ship is pitching and rolling so much it's extremely difficult to move around. Finally, Wolfe and I couldn't wait any longer. We had to use the head and its location is right in the point of the bow. It was a grabbing hand-over-hand struggle to get there. As I reached for the door handle, a cry of distress pierced the wail and howl of the wind. Peering through the doorway neither of us were prepared for the sight that met our eyes.

Here was a GI laying flat on his back sliding all over a water covered, wildly pitching deck. His eyes were terror stricken and his face and hands were bloody. The problem was two big trash cans had broken loose while he was sitting on the toilet. The head was now a bowling alley and the toilets were the ten pins. Already four of the six hoppers were smashed into smithereens. Pieces of sharp porcelain were flying everywhere. This could have made a prize Hollywood comedy, but we weren't laughing. Shouting for help was useless so we went about the task of rescuing this poor fellow.

The urinal trough ran the width of the bow. So hand over hand we edged our way across the wet, slippery urinal trying to get to the more stable middle of the ship. Our forlorn buddy had managed to grab a hold of the last, lone hopper. Quickly, we reached out to grab him but, just as our hands touched, a flying can shattered it and his hold. Once again he was sliding in every direction. He was attempting to kick away the bigger pieces and at the same time he was strugging to get his pants up over his buttocks. Many times he slid right by us as we failed to hold with our wet hands. Finally, he slid right at us. Wolf got a boot and I got his hand. Ever so slowly we got him and his pants up and to the medics where he received bandages from head to foot.

Of course, when we returned to our bunks and told our tale everyone laughed. It was a needed diversion to get the storm off our minds. The foghorn is wailing every thirty seconds. To stay in our bunks we have to lay spread-eagled with our hands and legs braced against the adjoining bunks. Me and many others are thinking this ship can't continue to toss and bounce like this and stay together. I'm recalling news reports of Liberty ships that cracked open in high seas.

Now there's an ungodly groaning of metal scraping on metal. It rises to one crescendo and down to another. This is not helping Wolf's state of mind. I can tell by his strange silence.

That had to be the longest night of my life. Now the sun is out and it has brought back many smiles. The ocean is again calm but more fellows are sick. A rough sea doesn't seem to bother Wolf and me, but a rolling one makes me feel woozy. The prop was another matter. It was loudly going "flip flop, flip flop" followed by a whirling sound which vibrated the whole ship. We dashed back to the stern and found the prop more out of the water than in. Wolf quipped,

"The oars are still a good idea." On checking the posted map, our worst fears were founded. In the last 24 hours we traveled 40 miles. A crewman posted the Captain's latest bulletin.

"I'm sorry but I must cut the ships speed. It's necessary to prevent the possibility of losing the propeller." Already the "flip flop" is gone, so are the smiles. This ride is beginning to resemble the Army train trips.

Thursday, December 6th: Not only have we passed the halfway mark, but the Captain has announced that the calmer ocean will allow him to increase the prop to 72 R.P.M. He states that we should make port next Thursday, the 13th.

This really has been an educational trip watching Mother Nature change her looks. Yesterday the spray off the waves created the look of a desert sandstorm. Today it's a perfect mirror calm. The tremendous displays of lightning and then full rainbows, plus the nightly shower of shooting stars, has been an awe inspiring experience.   A Brown bird, followed by two seagulls, flew by today. It was only natural I offer my new opinion to the farm boy.   "We're closer to land than the map shows. The Captain is going to surprise us."

"Rags, just keep the oars ready."

The crew helped with a diversion today. They gave us a first hand tour of the ship's innards. All questions were given honest answers.

"Yes, the whole ship is welded."

"That's true. Liberty ships have cracked open."

"Oh, the last one I heard was last month in Alaska. They were lucky. The ship was docked."

"See this weld here? It's a cracked one." Wolf raised his hand with one finger protruding.

"Can we get the Chaplain now? I'd like a prayer for a week of calm seas."

****

Friday was a good day as the Sea Ashe logged 288 miles. Saturday was okay until the winds picked up. By midafternoon the hatches were secured and we were back on the cots confined to quarters. As we held on for life we noticed a new, good phase. It was getting much colder. For once I beat Wolf to the punch.

"Ollie, you have the first watch tonight. Be on the outlook for icebergs."

Sunday: There was little sleep last night and the gale winds are still whistling through the ship's lines. The waves are running extremely high so we are barely moving. At times it feels like we're going backwards. Yesterday's 30 miles seem to confirm that.

Monday, December 10: Our spirits are on a slow defensive rise tonight. Our docking port has been changed from Virginia to New York. The Captain is still hoping to dock Thursday. Our other woes are sour milk and spoiled meat. The guys with the runs and heaves have just about had it. We're praying the Captain's Thursday is right.

Tuesday: Last night it was another impossible night in the pits. Wolf and I had to make a necessary trip to the head. For the first time in our friendship we held hands. The bow seemed to be rising straight up. It would hesitate a few minutes and then come crashing down with a thunderous creaking sound. Upon hitting the water she vibrated like a pogo stick. Needless to say we didn't hang around the men's room longer than necessary. Wolfe was very observant.

"Rags, I think you need more practice. I don't think you ever hit the trough." Coming back we were really slow motion. We checked every welded joint for cracks.

Here it is Wednesday and New York is 350 miles due east. Our speed is two and a half knots which equates to another six days at sea. To boost morale the crew went ahead with the planned "farewell dinner." Wolf says they want to use it before it spoils. He may be right. Rumors have it that our food supply is almost out. We'll soon see.

This is Thursday, the 13th, our promised docking day. After breakfast I pulled my way up the stairs to take a peek out the little, door window at the top of the stairs that overlooks the bow. I almost lost another meal. We were going down hill at a 45 degree angle. For sure I thought we were a goner. All I could see was a mountain of water over my head. I ducked as it came crashing into the door. Struggling to my feet I looked again. Now we were headed straight up and I was staring into a cloudy, snow squalled sky. My knuckles were white as I held on awaiting the impending crash that had to follow. Enough was enough. I eased my way back to my bunk wondering when all this was going to end.

A meager supper time is over and, surprisingly, the ocean has calmed enough to allow a few more RPMs. The latest Captain's report states, "I'm hopeful of reaching New York on Saturday." We're familiar with that "hopeful" bit, but at least the ship has stopped it's groaning.

The young Captain just came by with a grin announcing,

"I'm going to full throttle. If the ocean stays calm, we can make port tomorrow. Sure enough, within minutes the ship and prop were making new noises. Wolf immediately whispered in my ear,

"You want to bet, Rags? My ten bucks sez the prop flies off."

On awakening Friday morning we were sailing quiet and smooth, too smooth. I dashed up the familiar stairs and stepped out into a new element — pea soup fog. A smiling sailor informed me we were so close we could swim to shore. He meant well, but the fog never lifted. We had another day of fog horn melody as the Sea Ashe continued its doggie paddle to New York.

There was utter stillness when I awoke Saturday. It was a weird feeling, no noise with little vibration. I nudged Wolf and hopped into my ODs. Rushing on deck I found we were barely moving on a fog-like lake. They informed us a pilot was trying to locate us.

Two hours later we inched our way foward. Every bit of rail space had a GI trying to spot land. Then, out of the fog, a small ship was coming right at us. Suddenly we realized it was decked out in flags and banners. "Welcome Home" appeared and the band struck up "The Stars And Stripes

Forever." The deck was lined with pretty girls waving little flags. We answered with a big cheer and waved back. Chills were running up and down my spine for this once in a life-time experience.

As the fog lifted, we moved on and then there she was, the Statue Of Liberty. Our shaky, twenty-day cruise was over. Wolf and I were back in the States.

****

Chapter 22

Home At Last

In the afternoon our bus was crawling through the heart of New York city. This was Wolf's first visit and comment.

"Sure doesn't look like any place I'd want to live. It looks worse than Europe, and it hasn't been bombed."

We were still in the Army. We didn't know where we were headed, but we had our choice of rumors. Wolf remarked,

"Just give me an Army cot that doesn't rock."

One of the rumors was naturally right. They ushered us into Camp Kilmer's neat mess hall, serving a real American meal, with the invitation, "Eat all you want." While eating, I spotted a PX across the street. I ran over and wrote Ginny another great telegram.

"Put up my stocking. I'm coming in on my nose and a prayer."

Sunday's breakfast was at seven. The Sgt. quietly said,

"At 9 a.m. you will stand full inspection. Everything from your duffel bag will be laid neatly on your bunk."

We had heard about these inspections. It wasn't about spit and polish. They were looking for non-allotted equipment and uniforms. The rules allowed us to bring home one foreign weapon. Naturally, many guys, especially Ordnance, were trying to beat the system.

In Passau the Company had captured a river barge which was loaded with new, Spanish replicas of the U.S.Colt 45. Everyone got one but I was also carrying a neat, little, antique French pistol that I had recovered during a round up in a German village. Its two barrels were powder and ball fired. I didn't want to lose this baby.

The guys were hiding their stuff everywhere; in boots, under the mattresses and in the toilet bowl. It was quite a dilemma. Finally, I wrapped it in my washcloth and stuck it in my little toilet bag with the toothbrush and soap. Then, of all things, Privates came in to do the inspections! They were really getting a kick in overturning our whole barracks in their hunt for treasure. When they finished they confiscated enough Ike jackets, shoes, shirts, blankets and weapons to arm and clothe a barracks of men. Happily, my toilet bag ploy outsmarted the rookies.

After a final physical we were told we would be split up by our different regions of the country. Wolf couldn't believe Ohio was in the east. In disbelief we ended up in the same barracks on the same twin bunks. They were never used. By dusk we were on a train to another "secret" base.

From experience I knew we weren't on the Pennsy road to Philadelphia. With all the excited chatter, it took me some time to wake up. This was the B&O line to Washington! This was the same railroad that I hiked as a kid. Despite the darkness I could tell we were going over the "Ninety Foot" bridge, which was the home of my old fishing hole. And, it also meant that in another mile I'd be passing within 500 yards of my home. As I excitedly told Wolf, I yelled, "Stop the train I want to get off!" Grinning, Wolf patted my leg and replied, "Over my dead body."

Two hours later our camp wasn't much of a secret. I was right back where I started from 39 months ago, Indiantown Gap. They marched the whole trainload into a huge hall. We liked the first words from the Major's mouth.

"Trust me, within forty-eight hours you will be deprocessed and on your way home." He also added our hours wouldn't be 9 to 5. How right he was. At 3:00 a.m. we got our supper.

Monday and Tuesday it was marching from one building to another. The GI Bill and the GI Insurance were explained in detail. A nice Lt., with promises of instant upgrades, tried to sell us on the merits of re-enlisting. Otherwise Wolf and I had lots of cot time to dream aloud about our futures. Late Tuesday evening we got the final news.

"All of your money and your discharge will be presented to you tomorrow, December 19."

It was past midnight and I was tired from all the late hours but, for some reason, I tossed in my sleep like a raw recruit.

The barracks were bitter cold in the morning and, as we marched to mess, it started to snow. What a perfect way to end an Army career, getting home for the holidays and a white Christmas to boot.

An hour later we had our mustering out check of $300, our discharge paper and a handshake. A young Colonel, in a brief ceremony, delivered a patriotic speech of thanks. His quick conclusion caught us by surprise.

"Gentlemen, you are officially misters. again. You are free to go. Merry Christmas and have a safe journey home."

In a slow wave everyone stood up and yelled. Wolf and I slapped one another around and then, coming to our senses, said, "Let's get out of here." Back at the barracks our packed bags were waiting. We picked them up, walked to the door, turned on our heels and gave a "so long" salute to our last Army cot.

In Harrisburg it was one o'clock when we walked into the crowded train station. It was snowing hard. All trains were late. It seemed like a miracle that Wolf and I had stayed together this long. Now it was time to say our goodbyes. We exchanged some silly thoughts, about getting married, and that we would stay in touch. Slapping one another on the back and shaking hands we said our final "So long."

Wolf appeared minutes later standing on the snow swept West platform while I stood on the East. He gave me a weak wave, then as time wore on and the cold set in, we were giving one another weak shrugs. His train came first and in a few minutes it was loaded and moving out. Standing there I was transfixed. Presto, the loaded platform was empty and Les Wolf, after all these years, was gone from my life. My mind flashed back to Junior Levis. He, too, was from Philadelphia but he's lying in France. I was lucky and grateful that I was standing on this snowy platform.

I managed a window seat in the first car. Soon I would be seeing familiar places. My excitement was growing. Then it was snowing so hard I couldn't see past the window. The whistle was blowing worse than the foghorn. How could the engineer see? I wanted a fast ride but this looked and sounded as apprehensive as a day on the ocean.

An hour later the snow let up just as the Philly skyline came into view. Getting off at the North Philly station I knew the long walk to the Broad Street subway. Then it was a short twelve minute ride to catch the 26 trolley. I was hoping I wouldn't meet anyone I knew. This was a moment I wanted to savor, riding up the avenue, thinking about the old neighborhoods.

The car was half empty and I was the only military guy on board. Just as I settled down there came a tap on my shoulder. Turning I faced a stranger.

"Where you coming from soldier?"

With a smile I nonchalantly said, "Europe."

"Welcome home, son, and a Merry Christmas." He kept asking questions until a mile from my stop. I was grateful, he made a slow trip seem faster.

As I got off at Bleigh Street, I was aware that I was hoisting my heavy duffel bag for the last time. The final hike wasn't going to be easy. Five inches of snow had fallen and home was a long four blocks. As I passed the butcher shop, the memories started to flash back of all the times I had skated here, kettle in hand, to pick up the fresh sour kraut. Next, was the great, penny candy store from early school days at Crossan which was across the street. Now for some reason it looked a lot smaller. The barber shop windows were steamed up. Selke's old garage clock said three thirty, and I still hadn't seen a single person. Rounding the Lawndale Avenue corner I could feel my heart pounding, and I knew it wasn't the load on my shoulder. It was strange but for some reason these houses seemed smaller too and the street was narrower. The old homestead was now in view. The only footprints in the snow were mine. It was a perfect homecoming and the set up for a complete family surprise.

I turned into our sidewalk, noticing how large the trees had grown, and set my duffel bag down alongside the house. Sneaking across the porch I rang the door bell and then dashed for the back door. During the day the door was always unlocked. Quietly, I sneaked into the shed and peeked into the kitchen. Just as I had figured pots were on the stove with mixing bowls on the table. Little did Mom realize she was starting my supper. Now poor Mom was answering the door bell. Stepping into the kitchen I heard Pop holler from below,

"Who's at the door, Mame?"

Before she could answer she spotted me.

"Oh, you son of a gun! You little stinker you!'

This had to be one of the oddest Mother's greetings of all time. Pop heard my laugh and came charging up the cellar stairs. A lot of hugs and handshakes, with a few tears, went the rounds. For sure I was home and everyone was experiencing that great family feeling. As things settled down, Mom asked, "Does Ginny know your home?"

"Not exactly, but she will in a few minutes."

Ginny lived three blocks to the east and they could easily spot anyone coming around the southern corner. I put my war knowledge into play taking the longer, north route across Shelmire Avenue. My hunch paid off. As I turned down Montour Street, there she was, with her back toward me, shoveling snow. Making like an Indian I dashed from tree to tree until I was twenty feet behind her. I couldn't believe my ears, she was singing, "Let it snow, let it snow."

I stepped out and walked right up behind her and in my Clark Gable voice quietly asked,

"Can I help you, Miss?"

The reply was an instant scream, which coincided with an overwhelming female charge. This rugged soldier was shaken to his foundation from the avalanche of hugs and kisses. What a welcome home. When I got my second breath I asked,

"Can I go around the block? I'd like to try that one more time!"

The next morning I walked across the street and pulled the pillow from under Brog's sleeping head. Then it was down the block for a great reunion with Ed Perry. Everything was falling into place except for one minor detail.

Christmas eve was only four nights away. My work was cut out. In a new pair of gloves Ginny found a ring. I had learned fast. I braced myself for the scream and I was perfectly resigned for the ensuing female charge.

Eight months later, on a hot August night, Ginny finally got around to giving me my ring. Now it's 1994, and we are living happily ever after, proving it's okay to rob the cradle as long as you pick the right one.

****

Chapter 23

Epilogue

Friendships can be fickle and time takes a toll. My Army friendships went that route. For a few years the Christmas cards were exchanged faithfully but marriages, moves and growing families, took its toll. Wolf was one exception. In 1948 we paid the family a visit on their Oak Harbor farm in Ohio. Wolf married four years later. Then slowly, for unknown reasons, all correspondence ceased.

Suddenly, time flew; it became 1980! I was laid up with a strained back. To cheer me up Ginny went in the attic and brought me a stack of old Army letters. As I read, I began to wonder about those friends. Where and how were they? Had life treated them well? I picked up the phone and called Wolf. His bewildered wife answered me.

"Les died in 1967; he was only forty-six."

This news really shocked me and I had second thoughts about making any other calls. But, if anyone could bring a laugh, Art Doggett would. He wasn't to be found in his old home town of Baltimore. Playing phone detective I finally found Arthur in Verona, Kentucky.

Dogs first words were, "Where the hell you been, boy?" It was like old times. Art told me the 83rd had held a reunion every year since 1946. In a month the reunion was coming to Philadelphia.

"You better get your northern ass there!"

Five of us—Dog, Bond, Phillips and Appleby—attended. It was such a great experience; it seemed like time threw us back forty years. Nobody had changed! I went right back to the phone and in a short space of time I found one hundred and twenty five of the Company. Friendships quickly blossomed as the fellows came to the yearly reunions. Now across the country we were visiting one another and rebuilding those treasured friendships.

Gene Bond's finger never healed. He got over his friend in Luxembourg and came home single. A decade later he married Jane and became a meat inspector for the state of Michigan. We were great golf partners at the reunions for five years. Sadly, Gene died of a heart attack in 1986.

Charlie Rohrer owned two successful lumber and concrete yards in Ohio. Charlie lost two wives to illness before finding Pat. His problem now is smiling Pat can beat him at his own game...golf.

Ivan Gilman, our "Dear Lt.", traveled world wide as an executive officer with Chevron Oil working up international contracts. We're still trying to upstage one another with tongue in cheek letters. Ivan and Pat have become true, long distance, friends.

Good buddy Vin Musser has had a tough life. On returning home he was stricken with a mental disorder. Shock treatments wiped out his talents as a jeweler and also all memory of the war. I refound Muss, an Ohio boy, in 1987 reunited with his family in California. Muss only remembered being seasick and the name Rags. We have stayed in touch.

George Harris, our good section leader, owned the main lumber yard in Williamsport, Pa. Nice visits have been shared with George and Mettie. At 85 he still looks forward to seeing everyone at the reunions.

Big Jim Jones had an Army career that lasted until the early seventies. In all he had 33 commands. He impressed us by his ability for remembering every one of us. His grinning explanation, "There was only one World War II!" Our tough 1st Sgt. has become a caring friend.

Another fellow also made himself quite an Army career. Joe Brown achieved the rank of Colonel. He was always well liked for his even, quiet leadership. He is still quite a gentleman.

Arthur Doggett is still happily married to Milly his seventeen-year-old Camp Atterbury bride. I'm not so sure about Milly. Art honored the 783rd by becoming the 83rd's National President. With Ginny, the four of us have enjoyed a second lifetime of friendship.

Of the 150 men that made up the 783rd in Europe at least 67 of them have stood their last retreat. Lt. Knoerl was our armament officer at Atterbury when he transferred to the Air Force. In 1985 I reached his family only to discover that he went down with his P-51 in 1944.

At the Kentucky reunion in 1983 Jim Jones summed up our feelings of this Army experience. It was early morning, on a cloudless day; eight of us were standing, waiting on the first tee of this beautiful golf course to tee off. Jim quietly looked at each of us before speaking.

"Who of us could have imagined, back in the Normandy hedgerows, that forty-five years later, we'd be standing here to enjoy a round of golf?... Isn't this one great feeling?"

I believe a great lesson has been learned. Old friendships never die. There's always a glowing ember. It can be re-kindled, most times all that is needed is the breath of your phone call.

****

June 6, 1994

Fifty years in itself is a lifetime. Over such a long period of time one can forget a lot. Such is not the case on returning for the first time to the European battlefield. It was naturally, excitingly interesting to be a part of the 50th anniversary.

One can never forget the terrain of Omaha Beach or that long climb up to your first hedgrow. Likewise Carentan and Ste. Mere Eglise, village wise, still look the same. The surrounding country side has fewer hedgrows and that "fresh" farm odor is missing.

Two things struck me. The gratefulness of the people, young and old, through France, Belgium and Luxembourg. In Sainteny, France, the whole town of 750 people turned out on a Sunday morning to greet, honor and wine and dine us. The celebration went on for six hours as various people, in broken English, would say, "Thank you for giving us our freedom."

On visiting four cemeteries and viewing the physical number of crosses, one couldn't help but become emotional. I found Jr. Levis' grave and, after a few proper words, I gave him his deserved salute. As I was turning away, I passed by a grieving woman wailing at a cross. I heard her final words as she got up and walked away.

"Why, why, why? It was all in vain?" Her distressed feelings are understandable for up until a few years ago they could have been my words. There has to be a better way of settling disputes than war. But, in the past few years we have seen the Berlin wall come down as the people in Africa, the Middle East and Russia earned their freedoms.

Sadly, our American freedom was won on the carnage of the Civil War. Europe's was won with World War II. I left the cemetery of the true, war heroes, humble and quiet, now knowing that the Jr. Levises of this war had not died in vain.

Acknowledgments

Every book is like a life. You can't do it alone. Les Wolf's son Ron, as a tribute to his Dad, has made this book possible. Any wording of "Thank you" is inadequate.

Behind every married author is a wife. I'm grateful that Ginny managed to stand straight and tall in spite of the barrage of questions I threw at her.

For simplicity's sake I centered in on just a few of my closest everyday friends of the 783rd. In reality many of you are written about but unnamed. To all my good friends—

Phil Barbara, Steve Blasko, Bob Burns, Q. Boyette, Jim Christian, Paul Bryars, Gene DelPrete, Ray Downing, Jim Foster, Carl Frederick, Lloyd Grayson, Herman Hackstock, Bob Hammond, Easy Labbe, Bill Manning, Frank Salontay, Ed Perko, Joe Hendrix, Ray Wiggins, Al Unfried, Hersch Weaver, Al Bensimon, Troy Bishop, Percy Mohon and John Forster—I am grateful. All of you have brought these pages to life making the "War Years" and the "Golden Years" the learning experience of a lifetime.

I must also tip my hat to Ivan Bud Gilman. His helpful criticism, memory and encouragement, "Let's get the damn thing done before everybody dies," kept me writing a few extra hours a day.

Some of you photographers are unknown but your photos will be remembered. And lastly, I'm indebted to Jeff Otto whose art skills and computer expertise put the professional touch to all the included maps, sketches and photographs.